THE
Changeling

a memoir of

my death and rebirth,

my haunted childhood,

and my education in

sainthood and sin

GAIL GALLANT

Doubleday Canada

Doubleday Canada and colophon are registered trademarks of Penguin Random House Canada Limited.

Library and Archives Canada Cataloguing in Publication

Gallant, Gail, author

The changeling: a memoir of my death and rebirth, my haunted childhood, and my education in sainthood and sin / Gail Gallant.

Issued in print and electronic formats.

ISBN 978-0-385-68656-3 (softcover).—ISBN 978-0-385-68657-0 (EPUB)

1. Gallant, Gail. 2. Authors, Canadian (English)—21st century—Biography. 3. Sisters—Death. 4. Grief. 5. Autobiographies. I. Title.

PS8613.A459376Z46 2019   C813'.6   C2018-904935-9

C2018-904936-7

Cover images: Photos courtesy of the author; (frame) Irina Maslova / Alamy Stock Photo; (linen) Annie Spratt / Unsplash

Book design: Rachel Cooper

Printed and bound in the USA

Published in Canada by Doubleday Canada,
a division of Penguin Random House Canada Limited
www.penguinrandomhouse.ca

10 9 8 7 6 5 4 3 2 1

Penguin
Random House
DOUBLEDAY CANADA

For Michael

PROLOGUE

I'D BEEN IMAGINING MYSELF BEING PUNCHED IN the face for a long time now. It happened daily, and always caught me by surprise. Only when I was alone. A disembodied fist. The bones of my right cheek compressed on impact. The blow as cool as a breeze.

That wasn't all. I often imagined a long knife being plunged neatly into the middle of my chest. No one appeared to be holding the handle. A suspended knife; a sudden single thrust. There was no blood. There was never any pain. Only an intense adrenalin-spiked rush. It felt good.

By all appearances, I was managing well. I was thirty-three years old, with an enviable job at the Canadian Broadcasting Corporation (CBC), a seemingly solid marriage and a beautiful, bright young son. But privately, I felt my entire life had been a catastrophic mistake, a secret sham. I judged my days by how successfully I avoided crying in public. I kept a small notepad in my purse and spent my commute scribbling in it for solace. *I am living in a wonderland of ghosts.* And sometimes literally scribbling—long horizontal lines from left to right, evenly spaced one below the other, filling up page after page. Other times, I wrote about myself in the third person: *She'd like to sleep and never wake up.*

I was a changeling, switched at birth with a baby who had died. Torn between my two identities, I was neither. I was no one.

Linda, my mother, Glenna and
my father at Gail's funeral.

My First Communion.

PART 1

ANGEL

ON FRIDAY, JULY I, 1955, LAWRENCE GALLANT LEFT work a few hours early, a special treat to kick off his vacation. He and Maria packed the car, hoping to get out of the city before the afternoon rush hour. It was the same vacation they'd taken every summer since they'd moved to Toronto from Prince Edward Island eight years earlier. Same destination, same route, same excitement. Their annual road trip back home.

Every summer holiday brought another opportunity to catch up with old friends and family, and to show, yet again, Maria's once-doubting father that her marriage to Lawrence hadn't been a mistake. This year, the couple had three young daughters on display. Along with four-year-old Linda and two-year-old Glenna, their family now included newborn baby Gail.

This trip would also break in their brand new car, a turquoise Ford Fairlane with a broad band of chrome. Lawrence was looking forward to driving down the ferry dock ramp in Cornwall on the south shore of PEI and showing it off to relatives living in Summerside and the tiny towns and villages along the red dirt roads on the west end of the island.

Maria had been preparing for weeks. She'd picked through the girls' summer clothes, mending, washing and ironing. She'd ordered a few new print dresses from the Sears catalogue. She always ran her family on the tightest of budgets, but for vacations down home, her daughters had beautiful dresses, the dresses of her own childhood dreams.

For the long drive east, baby Gail was bundled between her parents in the front seat, a typical arrangement in the days before car seats. Linda and Glenna were in the back. Maria had packed the cooler with cold chicken sandwiches wrapped in wax paper, soda pop, apples and sugar cookies. There were dolls and books for the girls, and beers for Lawrence. In the early evening, they ate picnic-style on a blanket spread out on the ground off to the side of Highway 401, cars whizzing by.

Lawrence planned to drive straight through the night, which meant they would arrive on the island by dinnertime Saturday. At 10:30 that evening, Linda was still awake and restless, so Maria reached into the backseat and passed her a rosary.

Maria was just drifting off to sleep herself when the crash occurred. The impact was head-on. She hit the dashboard and landed on the floor on her hands and knees. Stunned by the blow to her head, she looked up through the shattered windshield at a wall of mangled metal, the car's front hood. She could hear screams from the backseat. She saw Lawrence's right arm flailing above her, reaching back to Linda and Glenna. Slowly, Maria began to realize what had happened. Blood, glass and broken bones. Her baby was gone.

Maria found Gail, still wrapped in her blanket, on the floor. She tried to reach out but couldn't move her right arm. She cried out to Lawrence for help. He picked up the baby and laid her in Maria's left arm.

"Your face is cut," she heard him say. She felt nothing.

Lawrence struggled with his door but couldn't open it. He thought of gasoline and fire and reached desperately for the backseat door to let Glenna and Linda out, but it was stuck shut too. In a panic, he smashed out his window, slicing open his elbow.

Strangers from a nearby roadside diner began surrounding the car, yelling in French and tugging at the door handles until they finally opened. Linda and Glenna were pulled out, crying. Someone reached in and took the baby from Maria.

The family was helped into the diner. Lawrence couldn't walk on his right foot. His left arm was gashed. He was bleeding from his mouth. Maria's right arm was badly broken, and the right side of her face was cut open from her cheekbone to her jaw. She had a concussion. She was laid out on a table.

As they waited for the police and ambulance, Glenna, uninjured, scrambled like a frightened animal under the restaurant chairs, away from the well-meaning strangers. Linda was giddy and dazed, chatting non-stop to whomever would listen, holding up her baby finger to show that it was broken. A woman cradled Gail at a distance and tried, with gestures and broken English, to reassure Maria.

In a far corner, the other driver, who had drifted over into their lane, was slumped on a chair, barely scratched.

A doctor arrived with the ambulances and Maria begged him to bring Gail to her. Instead, he huddled over the infant on the other side of the restaurant. When he finally brought Gail closer, her head was covered with a large bandage. Maria tried to reach out but the doctor wouldn't let her touch her baby. He said there was a minor abrasion on her head and he didn't want it to get infected.

Gail was placed in a separate ambulance from her family and taken to the Sainte-Justine's children's hospital in Montreal. Lawrence, Maria, Linda and Glenna were brought to the Hôtel-Dieu Hospital.

Maria was told she had a compound fracture in her arm that would require surgery to set properly. She objected, afraid of losing consciousness and missing word about Gail. Two doctors reluctantly took hold of her as she lay in the bed, forcefully wrenching her shoulder and broken arm into realignment so they could apply a cast. The pain was blinding. Next, a doctor spent hours sewing the wound on her face shut, edging his way along the gash as he picked out tiny fragments of glass. She would never believe he'd found them all.

The next two days were a nightmare, feverish and chaotic. The family stayed together in one hospital room. The girls were traumatized and Glenna was particularly difficult, stricken with diarrhea and impossible to control. Linda emptied her mother's purse and dripped nail polish all over the hospital bed. Maria could only think of Gail.

After two days, the family was discharged, but they were told baby Gail would have to remain behind at Sainte-Justine's. Her head injury was too severe to risk a hospital transfer to Toronto.

Lawrence and Maria knew no one in Montreal. They barely spoke any French, and they couldn't afford to pay for accommodations. They were encouraged, for now, to return home to Toronto. Little Gail would be in good hands. The local police arranged for a berth on a train heading west that evening. Covered in bandages, in casts and on crutches, they took their two older daughters and left Montreal without their baby.

⤙

In the days that followed, weak and burning with pain, delirious with anxiety, Maria spoke with the hospital daily. Gail's condition was still listed as critical. X-rays had confirmed a skull fracture that would require brain surgery. Maria and Lawrence were asked to return to Montreal as soon as possible to sign a letter of consent.

The couple, still in excruciating pain, left Linda and Glenna in the care of an aunt and took the train back to Montreal. When they looked down at baby Gail, pale and bandaged in a hospital cot, they were devastated. Lawrence was overcome with emotion and had to leave the room. Maria sang sweetly through tears until Gail's eyes fluttered and slowly opened. When she saw her mother, her lower lip began to tremble.

They had hoped to stay for the surgery, but it was delayed. For a second time, Lawrence and Maria were forced to leave Gail and return home to their other daughters in Toronto.

Later that week, the surgery was finally performed. Gail's surgeon sounded cautiously optimistic. "Time will tell," he said on the phone.

Through the long hot days of late July, Maria struggled to care for Linda and Glenna, praying hourly for the baby to be well enough to come home soon.

Gail had been in the hospital for two weeks when her parents were notified that she was to be discharged. They were overcome with relief and joy. Maria bought a pink frilled baby-doll dress and a matching bonnet for her daughter's homecoming.

The next day, Lawrence and Maria were waiting for the taxi that would take them to the train station when the phone rang. It was Gail's surgeon. Overnight, Gail's condition had changed dramatically. She had developed a high fever and was having convulsions.

Now they travelled back to Montreal in a fog of anguish, numb with disbelief. At the hospital, dressed in cotton gowns and masks, they looked down at their baby's face in cherubic repose. She was comatose.

Gail had contracted bacterial meningitis. Lawrence and Maria were told that all they could do now was wait and pray. They waited and prayed. After several days, with Gail's condition unchanged, they were forced to leave Montreal without their daughter for the third time. The parting felt unbearable.

In the two weeks that followed, baby Gail's condition slowly deteriorated. Maria staggered to daily Mass, prayed for hours at a time, cried, and begged God not to take her child. She was locked in a desperate negotiation. She asked him what she had done that her baby should be made to suffer like this. Why take this innocent life as punishment? She became more weak and gaunt and distraught by the day. Finally, the parish priest who had borne witness to Maria's agony put a hand on her frail shoulder and suggested it might be best to let Gail go back to God. Maria felt a sharp sense of release, a jagged exhale.

Gail died two days later, on August 15, 1955. She was buried in her coming-home outfit. Maria and Lawrence had wanted to mark her grave with an angel, but when the beautiful statue they'd ordered arrived, they were told it violated the cemetery's height restrictions. They were forced to settle for a modest stone set flat in the ground, etched with an angel's profile.

Over the next month Maria sank into a deep depression. She barely ate or slept. Lawrence, worried about the state of his wife's body and mind, asked the family doctor to make a house call. Despite the two small and bewildered girls at Maria's feet, the doctor suggested that having a new baby to care for might ease her pain.

Maria was seized by a thought. The doctors hadn't been able to save her baby's life. But with God, all things were possible. She began to pray desperately, feverishly, for a miracle. Gail was now an angel with God in heaven. In her prayers, Maria asked God for Gail's return.

A month later, she learned she was pregnant.

⤙

One afternoon in late November, still early in Maria's pregnancy, several neighbours came over to confront her about the fanciful tale Linda was telling the other children on the street—that her baby sister Gail who had died that summer was coming back.

The neighbours were concerned about Maria's mental health. She had lost a child, and they were sympathetic. But they were uneasy about the dramatic claim she was making to her two little girls, a story their own children were now bringing home.

"Suppose you give birth to a boy?" they asked. "What will you tell them then?"

"I don't need to suppose," Maria calmly assured them. "I'm having a girl."

⤳

It was late July the following year, after midnight, when Maria's water broke. Lawrence stayed home with the two children while she took a taxi to the hospital alone. She had not seen a doctor since the visit that confirmed her pregnancy. Those nine months had been uncommonly trouble-free, and even now, she felt no discomfort. Her lack of pain began to make her anxious—her first three deliveries had begun so differently.

She was admitted to the hospital at 3:30 a.m. A doctor examined her and told the nurse to take Maria straight to the delivery room. She was fully dilated, and the baby's head was already crowning. Maria laughed out loud in disbelief. She felt nothing.

In those days, women were often given a short-term general anesthetic in the final minutes of labour. The anesthetist paced the room, waiting for a contraction to cue him. But Maria lay still. He amused himself by singing "Jimmy Crack Corn" and joked that if the baby wasn't born by four o'clock, he was going home.

Maria felt a strange sensation spread across her abdomen, "like pins and needles," she told the doctor. He examined her again and signalled to the anesthetist that it was time.

"Since everything else is going your way, what do you want?" the doctor asked Maria.

"A seven-pound, nine-ounce, dark-haired baby girl," she said.

Those words were her last memory before she woke up twenty minutes later to find me lying in a bassinet beside her, my eyes wide open. Even the doctor agreed it had been a miracle. Maria had just given birth, without labour pain, to a dark-haired, dark-eyed daughter weighing seven pounds, nine ounces—a daughter who bore an uncanny resemblance to baby Gail.

2

REBIRTH

WHEN I WAS FIVE MONTHS OLD, I DIED. A YEAR later, I was reborn. Or so my mother said.

I only understood this fully when I was four years old. It was a crisp and sunny spring morning. From the window over the kitchen sink, we could see the backyard right down past the pear trees. My mother said they were beginning to bud. I was sitting at the table next to her. She held Jeannie on her lap. Linda and Glenna were at school. I loved these peaceful weekdays, just me and my mother and my baby sister. I could talk with my mother all day long. Jeannie wasn't old enough to join in.

The kitchen table, part of a metal dinette set with chrome trim and red vinyl chair seats, felt cool on my forearms. My legs dangled above the black-and-white checkerboard linoleum-tiled floor. There was a crucifix over the kitchen doorway, and an oval-framed picture of the Virgin Mary on the high-gloss turquoise wall. The milky smell of Jeannie's lumpy Pablum permeated the kitchen air, and her baby legs kicked out in happy anticipation at the sight of each spoonful.

I was listening to my mother, who was reminiscing about the moment she saw me in the hospital bassinet by her side.

"Your eyes were wide open, looking all around the room, just as though you'd been here before," she said. "Just like this."

She rolled her grey eyes up and about the kitchen, left and right, bright and confident, not like a newborn baby at all. She laughed, and I laughed too. Her skin was pale against her thick dark hair, and her face was tighter on the left side because of her long white scar. It made her smile look a little crooked.

"You were identical to her in every way," she said.

I had been hearing fragments of my birth story as far back as I could remember—the labour-free delivery, the anesthetist singing "Jimmy Crack Corn," but this time was different. Perhaps I'd finally been weaned on just enough Catholicism to recognize a miracle story when I heard one.

"God brought me back?"

My mother smiled coyly.

"Well," she said, "that's certainly how it looked."

Did she fear it would have been audacious, blasphemous even, to speak the words directly? *God performed the ultimate miracle, a resurrection, just for me.*

Instead, she let the facts speak for themselves. She let me draw my own conclusions.

I was too young to understand the full implications of her story, to begin to imagine the dark grief she'd only glided over, or to reckon with her claim that God had acted so deliberately in my life, but I did understand one thing: I was special. And, more importantly, I was special to my mother. I was her miracle child. The weight of this knowledge left me breathless, like being presented with the most precious gift from the most important person in the entire world.

⤙

My mother was the nerve centre of our house. My father was quiet and shy, distant and hard-working. He was rarely at home. She was the undisputed boss who kept all of us, including my father, in line and on the path of righteousness.

She had been educated at a residential convent school, and she would have made a perfect Mother Superior herself, with an intimidating demeanour and high moral standards. She lectured and instructed us, clothed and fed and nursed us. She was a natural disciplinarian who could frighten us with her anger. I remember no hugs and kisses, no sentimental tones. The word *love* was never uttered. But my mother showed her approval silently and subtly, and seeing her face relax and brighten was my greatest joy.

Throughout my preschool years, I'd sit at the kitchen table while my mother prepared dinner, or in the living room as she stood ironing our clothes, and listen, enthralled, as she shared anecdotes about the car accident, the other Gail's death and my birth. I asked questions, and was riveted by every detail. I was beginning to grasp the full circumstances of my life: the horror of the car accident, the severity of my parents' injuries, the reason for my mother's scarred face. I began to understand that I was a special gift from God to my mother, on account of her great faith in the face of her terrible loss. And my painless birth was an additional act of kindness on God's part, as though, in giving my mother back her dead baby, there was the solemn recognition that she had already suffered enough. It just wouldn't have been fair to make her endure a normal course of labour to deliver the same baby twice.

The family photo album provided the main evidence of the miracle story. There was a picture of my parents in casts and on crutches against floral-patterned wallpaper. There was the photo taken in the funeral home too, Glenna in my father's arms, Linda standing at my mother's side, both sisters staring vacantly at the photographer while our parents faced the little white casket set up between them. And there was the photo of a gravestone set flat in the ground, with an image of an angel in prayer. *In Memory of Our Darling Baby* was etched across the top, and my name, *Gail Gallant*, appeared below. I had been in that car accident too. I had died.

But the most arresting picture was framed and displayed on top of the TV set, placed inside the starched doily against a beautiful arrangement of plastic flowers. It was a colourized photograph of my father, holding a tiny baby girl in his arms. Printed with a shaky hand in ink in the upper right corner of the photo was *Gail Gallant at 3 months*. Once I was old enough to recognize my name in print, my mother had to correct my assumption.

"No, that's the other Gail."

This was the only picture of the other Gail in the house, and the most compelling proof that she had actually existed.

I couldn't remember my first birth but I gradually came to remember my second. My mother recounted the death and birth stories so often that I began to recall the events first-hand. The details filled me with a sense of pride and purpose. I didn't know anyone else who had died and then been born again. If I wanted to keep my mother happy with me, being her one and only reborn child was the key.

3

ANOINTED

"DO LINDA AND GLENNA KNOW ABOUT THE CAR accident?"

Jeannie was down for her afternoon nap. I was watching my mother pull Jeannie's clean cloth diapers, one at a time, from an overflowing laundry basket, fresh off the backyard clothesline, and fold them into perfect rectangles. She stacked them one on top of the other, building a soft white tower on the living room chesterfield.

"Yes, of course," my mother said, seemingly amused by the question. "They were in the car."

"But do they know about *me?*"

"Yes, of course they do."

That surprised me. It had been a few days since I'd fully grasped the supernatural circumstances of my birth, and I wondered why my mother was the only one who'd ever discussed it with me. My father never had much to say at home, but my sisters were normally so chatty. Just not about this. They certainly didn't treat me as if I were special. At least, not in a good way.

Linda was the classic first-born child, a little adult. She was sensitive, conscientious and responsible, with my father's handsome face and dark colouring.

Glenna was small for her age, fair-haired and thin. She was also bright and imaginative, but sandwiched as she was between Linda and two Gails, the middle-child curse was magnified for her. Until she was school-aged, she sought companionship in a coterie of imaginary friends.

Both sisters made me feel as though there was something different about me, but Linda, always on her best behaviour, surpressed her resentment. I looked up to her because she acted so grown up. Glenna's feelings were more transparent. Every year, her inventory of my flaws seemed to expand. She made fun of my boney rib cage until I cried and became convinced I was deformed. She drew attention to my scraggly hair, which made me look "like a witch." My eyes were too far apart—they gave her the creeps. My kneecaps were knobby.

If they really knew the truth about my miracle rebirth, why didn't they like me more? Maybe they didn't realize that I knew. Maybe they thought it was supposed to be a secret. It took me a few more days to build up the courage to raise the topic with them. It was a Saturday morning, and my mother needed to polish the kitchen floor. We were shooed out into the backyard until she was done. Linda and Glenna were together on the grass, occupied with their dolls. I sat on the pavement closer to the back door, bored, poking a stick into the grass. I could hear the loud motor of the floor polisher starting up inside. I waited a minute longer, then nervously broached the subject.

"Mom says that after the other Gail died, she prayed to God to bring her back, and then I was born."

They both looked over at me but said absolutely nothing. I pressed on.

"And I look just like her."

"Yeah, I know," Linda finally said, and returned to concentrate more intently on her doll.

"So?" Glenna muttered, and then looked away. I felt embarrassed. I could tell this was going nowhere, and besides, it was bragging, and I was old enough to know that bragging was wrong. But whatever my mother saw in me, my older sisters obviously saw something less. I regretted even mentioning it. I stood up, dusted off my pants, stuck my head inside the back door and yelled above the floor polisher.

"Mom, can I come inside?"

⤙

"Hurry up, Glenna," my mother huffed. "Don't forget to pack your socks. You'll need them on the road."

Glenna was standing at the bed, struggling to stuff a top and a pair of pants into a small bag as my mother stood over her. Looking down the whole time, Glenna moved slowly toward her dresser, feeling for a pair of socks in the drawer. She found some and pulled them out. She dragged her feet back to the little bag on the bed. Once she had stuffed the pair of socks inside, my mother marched her, holding onto her bag with both arms, down the hall to the front door. I scrambled out of their way as they passed by.

Linda and I took up positions in the living room, a few feet away from the front door entrance, and watched with mounting apprehension.

My mother opened the front door and looked down at Glenna, shrinking below her.

"Well? What are you waiting for? Go on." Her voice could chill a room. "Leave if you want to leave. Go ahead. Don't forget to write."

Glenna, head down, clutching her little bag, stepped reluctantly onto the front porch. She was just turning around—perhaps to apologize—when the door shut behind her.

In the front hallway on the other side of the door, my mother stood waiting and listening. Her face was stony with resolve. And then I heard it. Glenna had begun to cry. I felt a rising panic. *Open the door! Quick, let her back in!*

How long did my mother let Glenna cry on the other side of the door? A minute? Three? I don't know. It seemed too long.

"Are you ready to come back inside?" Her voice was frosty. I remember being shocked and confused.

Many years later, Glenna told me why she was being taught a cruel lesson that day. She had told our mother she hated me.

It was because I got all the attention. She no longer wanted to live with me.

"Then I guess you'll just have to leave," our mother had said.

I suspected from the beginning that I was an object of resentment, even before I could imagine why.

⤸

My own earliest memory is of sibling jealousy—a foggy, dreamlike memory of a memory about Jeannie's birth. I was two and a half years old. The day Jeannie was brought home from the hospital, my aunt Josie visited us. Josie sat on the couch and held Jeannie on her lap, cooing at her and admiring how pretty she was. I can remember watching from the other side of the living room until I couldn't stand it anymore. I ran out of the room, flying past my aunt, but not before landing a kick with my hard little shoe in the middle of her shin. I remember feeling seized by terrible shame and guilt before I'd made it halfway down the hall.

Over time, I grew to appreciate that Jeannie wasn't a threat but a teammate. I'd felt like an outsider around Linda and Glenna. But sweet, good-natured Jeannie became my first friend. We were kindred spirits. And since I was older, I took it upon myself to entertain her, to explain things to her, to set her straight. I always did most of the talking.

But the sibling rivalry for my mother's attention and

approval persisted, and would shape all of our lives in disparate ways.

⤙

We never knew our maternal grandmother. She died when my mother was only eight years old. But my mother told me that she'd been her mother's favourite child. It was understandable, because she was the only daughter in a family with seven sons, and she excelled at school. One day in early August, during the Great Depression, her mother took her to the annual summer picnic at St. Anthony's Parish near Summerside. Her mother entered a shooting-range contest and won a large doll for her daughter, the first doll she'd ever owned. It had a delicate porcelain head and a beautiful face, and was, Maria thought, the most perfect doll in the world.

In order to keep it safe when Maria wasn't playing with it, her mother hung it high up on a hook above the woodstove in the kitchen. One morning, they walked into the kitchen and found that the doll's delicate head had been smashed in with an iron poker. They never discovered which brother did it.

My mother told me that one or two of her brothers might have been jealous of her because she got so much of her mother's attention. If you are different, if you are special, someone will resent you. It's only natural.

⤫

One Sunday after church, my family sat around the kitchen table eating lunch. Linda and Glenna began talking about middle names, and we went through everyone in the family, listing them off. Linda casually mentioned that the other Gail's middle name was Marie. I felt my face go warm with surprise and embarrassment. I hadn't known our middle names were different. Marie sounded very close to my mother's name, Maria, and both of those names were very close to the Blessed Virgin's name, Mary. But *my* middle name was Bernice, after an aunt. It didn't make any sense. I much preferred the other Gail's middle name, and I didn't understand why Marie wasn't my middle name too. We were the same person, weren't we? We had the same first name. Why not the same middle name? But I was too timid to ask. I didn't say anything.

Everyone called me "Gail" and called her "the other Gail." Every time anyone referred to the other Gail, it gave me a tinge of pleasure mixed with an acute self-consciousness, as if I'd accidently overheard a compliment I wasn't meant to hear. No one else in my family had an "other" that was also the same. No one except me.

I studied the photo of the other Gail on top of the TV set. Her angelic face left me with mixed emotions, sad and grateful and slightly envious all at the same time. My sadness was for her suffering and death. My gratitude because her death was the reason I was special. And my envy was for her sacred shrine on top of the TV set—she was, there was no denying it, even more special than me.

When I looked for myself in her face, I found mystery instead, and a strange seed of confusion became lodged deep inside of me. It would gradually take root, and develop into uncertainty and a secret inner conflict.

Several years later, my mother walked into my bedroom one day and asked if I'd seen the picture of the other Gail. It was gone from the top of the TV set.

I was sitting on the side of my bed, legs dangling, and I looked up at her blankly. I shook my head. I had no idea what she was talking about.

She turned her back to me and opened the top drawer of my dresser. To my surprise, she found the framed photo inside, face down, hidden under my clothes. She held it up to me with an unhappy expression on her face. *How did that get there?* I wondered. I honestly couldn't recall having taken it. Yet I thought I *must* have taken it, and I was ashamed. It looked as if I'd been trying to hide the other Gail from her. But why would I do that?

My mother didn't say a word. She just looked at me a little longer, and then walked out of the bedroom, taking the picture with her. She didn't place it back on the top of the TV set. Instead, it was her turn to hide it. I stumbled across it many years later at the bottom of one of her drawers. She only brought it back out again after I had moved out of the house.

4

STIGMATA

OUR HOME WAS A TESTAMENT TO 1950S ROMAN Catholicism. There were crucifixes above the doorways and holy water fonts by the light switches in the bedrooms. There were framed pictures of Jesus, Mary and Joseph on the walls. There were medals on chains, and painted statuettes. The Blessed Virgin Mary—with her sad almond-shaped eyes, her immaculate heart exposed outside her chest and circled by a garland of tiny roses, flames rising toward her throat—*she* was my favourite. Her fingers demurely drew attention to her heart, to her precious pain, to her infinite sorrow. She kept an eye on me, watching from the wall outside my bedroom.

My mother's embrace of her faith went deep. She was born in 1931 in poverty in the rural west end of Prince Edward Island. Her father, Jack, had to struggle to support his family of ten. He was an intelligent man who loved to read, but he was also a depressive, drank too much moonshine and had a mean temper. Luckily for him, his wife, Lucy, was strong and strict and stable. When she died in 1938, Jack struggled to raise the children on his own, but the times were terrible and his already bad drinking habits worsened. As his seven sons became teenagers, they also began to drink, and to fight back. My mother, the only girl and second-youngest child, would describe those years as "almost unbearable."

Her life changed completely when she turned twelve. Her father used his war veteran's pension to send her to a convent school on the northwestern tip of the island. She went from being the only girl in a family with eight males to a Catholic all-girls boarding school. I always had the impression those nuns saved my mother's life, even if their words of comfort seemed cold: "God's will be done" and "You get what you deserve." At her graduation ceremony four years later, she was the class valedictorian.

Led by my mother, we said our prayers before meals and before bed, and we said the rosary as a family every evening during the forty days of Lent. We had rosary beads of many kinds and colours: pale blue and white and pink crystal beads, and black polished stones like teardrops. The rosary was the most direct link to the Blessed Virgin Mary, and Mother Mary had a direct link to God and her son Jesus.

Our family attended Mass at St. Bernard de Clairvaux Roman Catholic Church every Sunday morning. The church was a magnificent and magical place: the vaulted ceiling, the gilded sacristy, the ornate carved-wood confessionals, the melodramatic stations of the cross. I loved it all.

The sermon, the organ music, the incense and hymns, all built toward the rite of communion, the Eucharist. Stand, kneel, sit. Stand, kneel, sit. I revelled in the solemn repetition, the statues and stained glass and candle flames. I crossed myself with a delicate touch of my fingertips. Piety came naturally to me. The church was my second home.

On a Sunday afternoon when I was five, my family sat around the television in the living room and watched a movie called *The Song of Bernadette*. Bernadette was a sickly fourteen-year-old girl living in poverty in nineteenth-century rural France when the Blessed Virgin Mary began to appear to her, a rosary wrapped in her folded hands. For years, Bernadette suffered distrust, ridicule and humiliation because she alone could see the Virgin when she appeared. Bernadette was finally redeemed when pilgrims began to report miraculous cures at the site of the apparitions. I watched the movie enthralled, my eyes tearing up many times throughout.

I wanted to know more about apparitions of the Blessed Virgin Mary. For days, my mother happily discussed the topic with me. She knew a lot about almost everything, but especially about Roman Catholicism, and she explained the church's doctrine about miracles with confidence and authority. I was a captive audience. She told me all about Lourdes, in France, about Fátima, in Portugal, and about Sainte-Anne-de-Beaupré, a cathedral near Quebec City. These were all places where

Mary had appeared, mainly to women or girls, and which had become the sites of miracles thereafter.

"There have been hundreds and hundreds of miraculous cures," she said. "The cured leave their crutches and braces and wheelchairs behind as evidence, and because they don't need them anymore."

Then she told me something frightening. When the Blessed Virgin appeared to three children at Fátima, she gave them three secret messages for humankind. They were written down and kept safe in the Vatican, and were only revealed one at a time over many years. The first two were ominous warnings of future world wars, and the third called for the consecration of Russia. My mother explained that Russians didn't believe in God. The very thought was terrifying to me. It meant there was nothing to stop the Russians from committing terrible deeds, because they had no fear of eternal punishment. Atheistic Russia began to give me nightmares, but that wasn't the only fear that haunted me.

I began to wonder if I had been born again in order to fulfill some divine purpose. I knew that other people's babies died sometimes, but they stayed dead, and their souls went to heaven to be with God for eternity. But not my mother's baby. Not baby Gail. A gift this rare was bound to have strings attached. I would have to prove myself worthy. But how? Would I be called upon like the children at Fátima? Or like Bernadette? My middle name was Bernice, which began with the same four letters. Was that not an enormous coincidence?

Other children feared monsters and ghosts and bogeymen. At the age of five, I began to fear an apparition of the Virgin Mary. Like Bernadette, I felt a strong attraction to the Blessed Virgin. Surely it was only a matter of time before she visited and asked me to do something very difficult and courageous. I might be required to save some lives and become a world-famous martyr. I might be asked to convert Russia. Being anointed was a gift that brought with it crushing anxiety and pressure.

Outdoors, I searched the sky for signs, for visions, for suspicious rays of light cutting cracks through heaven's cloudy floor. I listened to the silence, waiting for a disembodied voice to call my name.

It was when I was lying in my bed at night that I was especially worried the Virgin would appear. Sometimes, I could almost make out her shape in the darkest corner of my bedroom. I wondered if she was checking up on me, holding back from appearing fully, watching and waiting until I was truly ready for my great mission.

In the washroom, I would sit on the edge of the bathtub and check the palms of my hands carefully for signs of the stigmata. Stigmata are another proof that a person is holy and chosen by God. These lesions appeared only on the hands and feet of very devout saints, matching Jesus's wounds from being nailed to the cross; sometimes, they even bled.

One day, I checked the bottoms of my feet. On the sole of my right foot, right in the middle, I found a pale brown freckle. I decided to keep an eye on it. If it started to ooze blood, I would have to tell my mother straight away.

I told no one about my fears of being destined for saint-hood or martyrdom. Neither my parents nor my sisters. I felt that Linda and Glenna would only ridicule me, and I worried that my mother would sense my fear. It seemed best to keep it to myself for as long as possible.

✤

I was deeply affected by the tragic stories and brutal imagery of my faith: Jesus nailed and hanging from the cross, thorns sticking into the skin of his forehead and drips of blood running into his eyebrows; Mother Mary's beloved son crucified before her eyes; countless saints and martyrs tortured to death because they refused to renounce their faith. These images of the terrible suffering and death of innocent victims felt very real and very raw. They struck close to home. Had I not suffered and died myself, when I was the other Gail?

But the tortured medieval religious icons and themes of sacred suffering in our home had stiff competition from a very different kind of melancholia. It was called country and western music, and it provided the anthems of our Maritime roots. In the early 1960s, we had a collection of record albums in cardboard sleeves with colourized photos of men and women in cowboy hats singing about personal heartbreak and failure and regret. Hank Williams. Patsy Cline. Hank Snow. Loretta

Lynn. Most of their songs were sad. I paced around the living room at a steady gait to the rhythm of Stonewall Jackson's tragic lyrics. The sting rose in my nose and my eyes teared. My throat hurt. There was so much sadness in the world. Things didn't end well.

Perhaps this is why I sometimes fainted. It happened the first time when I was about five years old. I was with my parents and sisters, saying the family rosary during Lent. We were on our knees on the carpet in the living room. As usual, my mother was leading the prayers, and we chimed in like a harmonic chorus around her. I became aware of a strange and beautiful feeling, a cool ticklish, prickly sensation on the back of my head. Darkness began to seep into the room from the outside edges of the ceiling like incense, and within seconds it had enveloped me. When the light came on again, my mother was lifting me onto the couch. I felt tired, like I'd been sleeping for a while, but perhaps not, because with the exception of my mother, everyone else was still on their knees. I had no understanding of what had just happened, only that my mother had rescued me, and I got to sit on the couch for the rest of the rosary that day.

I fainted a number of times after that, even during Mass at church. Eventually, I thought fainting easily was just another thing that was special about me. It didn't bother me at all. But if I was special, how much more so was my mother, who'd moved God to pity with her tears while all the other mothers cried in vain?

5

TRANSGRESSIONS

BY 1962, MY PARENTS HAD SIX CHILDREN, ALL UNDER
the age of twelve. Following Linda, Glenna, me and Jeannie
were Melanie, the tomboy of the family, and finally a real boy
named John, who was shy.

Being a middle child in our increasingly crowded little
bungalow added an additional layer of confusion to my identity. Although I believed my mother had a special relationship
with me because of my miraculous birth, I had less and less
of her time and attention with the arrival of each new sibling.
I stuck close to her side and engaged her as much as I could,
but she was preoccupied and exhausted by endless domestic
chores: the cooking and shopping, the scrubbing and vacu-
uming and polishing, the washing and folding and ironing.

Not that her life was all drudgery. When she was in a good
mood, we sat around the table at dinner enthralled by her

stories. She told us about her dreams, always strange and complicated adventures. She told us about Prince Edward Island when she was growing up—including ghost stories, like when she heard her mother's dying voice speak her name across the fields, calling her to her mother's deathbed, or the relative who saw a man recently dead walking along the road. She often gave us updates on her afternoon soap operas, her great indulgence. She would act out the soap's different roles, the characters' anger and shock and pettiness, their steady stream of flirtation, confrontation and melodrama. These were sinful people, and my mother followed their plot lines religiously.

When she was in a bad mood, she was silent as a stone. Her charcoal eyes smouldered. She could lower the temperature with the clench of her jaw.

⊥

There had been a great Maritime exodus in the 1950s, and dozens of my parents' close and distant relatives and friends now lived in Toronto. They transported their tradition of the kitchen party, with guitars and singing, to the basements of working-class neighbourhoods downtown.

I loved to watch my mother get ready to go out on a weekend evening, leaning over the bathroom sink, applying powder and rouge. Her dark, thick hair was teased and shaped with hairspray, and her deep-red lipstick was dramatic against her pale skin. She displayed little vanity and never preened or obsessed over her appearance, but she had plenty of pride. The nuns in the convent had trained her to stand straight and hold her head high, and I thought she looked like Queen Elizabeth. She rarely mentioned her long facial scar, though it could hardly be missed.

We children, with Linda acting as our official babysitter, stood in the living room window waving as the car backed out of the driveway, my mother looking regal in a floral-print dress with a crinoline skirt, and my father as handsome as a movie star with his Acadian features, his dark hair with a thick, wavy forelock hanging into his big brown eyes. Then we settled in for an episode of *The Saint* on TV, with a bowl of potato chips and cups of ginger ale.

At Sunday lunch the day after a party (after we'd returned from Mass), my mother would measure out scoops of baked beans, glasses of milk and slices of white bread and margarine and share her observations on the evening before. Ostensibly, she was speaking to my father, but he showed little interest in her remarks and rarely if ever responded to them. But I listened intently. My mother's party reports were how I learned about morality, particularly as it related to gender.

Her code of ethics was more medieval than biblical, more Seven Deadly Sins than the Ten Commandments. Selflessness, modesty, humility—these were key virtues, but her moral instruction largely centred on the importance of discipline and denial.

"There are men who drink too much because they are weak and lack self-control," she would say. "There are women who are desperate for attention and will do anything to get it."

Alcohol abuse and sexual promiscuity were reserved a special place in hell.

"Bridget got awfully tipsy. Did you notice?" she asked my father. He shrugged, barely looking up from his plate. "By the time she left she was slurring her speech."

"Annette has an awful lot of time for that fellow from O'Leary. Did you see how she threw herself at him? Charlie wasn't too happy about that." I wasn't sure I knew what Annette was up to, but I could tell it was no good.

"Annette had better watch herself. She'll find herself on the street."

The vivid characters and scenes she painted rivalled stories from her favourite soap operas.

"I don't know what's going to become of that Earl. A different girlfriend every time I see him, and each one's worse than the last. That latest is divorced with three kids."

My sisters and I were an eager audience, shuddering at every cautionary tale, solemnly processing each harsh lesson. Our mother's moral assessments were infallible. They were also entertaining.

That the church came with such a strict moral code focused particularly on the behaviour of women made sense to me. As far as I could tell from my own family, the salvation of the entire world depended on the strength of morally righteous women. My father might mean well, but he lacked my mother's fierce decisiveness and authority. And although he was more likely than my mother to show spontaneous moments of sympathy, he was largely absent from our young lives. He spent his days working hard in a factory, and when he came home, he just sat there, sullen and tired. He rarely engaged us.

Often, the day after a party, my mother would turn her critical eye on my father. He knew when it was coming and so did we. I could tell from the moment I got up in the morning, from the tension in the air, from the sounds my mother made with every plate she set down, every cupboard she closed, whether my father had been a saint or a sinner the night before. I dreaded those days when he'd disappointed her.

"You think I didn't notice how many times you disappeared behind the bar?" she would ask.

"I had three beers," he would mumble.

"Oh, please! Don't make me laugh."

It seemed to me that her most intense moral disapproval was reserved for my father's weekend drinking. When he got drunk at a social gathering, the effect on her was toxic. Her face became a pale, cold mask.

Our mother's childhood had been scarred by her father's heavy drinking, but Linda claimed that alcohol became an even bigger flashpoint after the car accident. Perhaps it was because the driver at fault had been drinking. Our father had always been a heavy social drinker, but after the accident, and as our family grew, his weekend drinking increased. He would drive home after a Saturday evening visiting relatives with an unsteady hand on the wheel while our mother braced herself in the passenger seat, fuming. It may not have been his intention, but he couldn't have found a more sure way to enrage and embarrass her if he'd tried. My father's weekend beer binges were one of the only things in our childhood that my mother couldn't control, and the only reason, as far as I knew, that they fought. But that proved to be plenty.

⟡

When my mother, at only seventeen years old, fell in love with my dad, her father thought his brilliant daughter deserved much better. My dad was shy, had little formal education, few job prospects, and had returned from his military training in Halifax, like many of his peers, a problem drinker. Alcohol was an effective anesthetic, and Lawrence Gallant had his own desperate childhood to live down. His father could be a mean man. Once, he shot my father's beloved dog in the head because it was barking. Unlike his own father, my dad was a gentle man. He chose to drown his pain instead.

Although I loved my father, I barely considered what he thought of me. I have so few early memories of our relationship. But I do have one. He took me to the dentist. I had several cavities that needed filling, and when the dentist's drill hit a nerve, I began to cry. He never offered a word of consolation, but he looked distressed, and on the way home, he stopped at the corner store for a pack of cigarettes. When he returned to the car he awkwardly presented me with a bag of candy. A whole bag of candy just for me, even though the side of my face was still throbbing. I knew my sisters would turn green when they saw it, and my mother would disapprove. But it was a gesture straight from his heart. My father had a notorious sweet tooth.

6

COMMUNION

WHEN I TURNED SIX, I BEGAN ATTENDING ST. FRANCIS
Xavier Catholic School. It was the first time I was away from
home during the day and, more importantly, away from my
mother. I hated it. She'd been the centre of my life, my sun,
and I felt completely hollowed out and abandoned without
her near me. I was intensely lonely in the crowd of strange
children. I missed my sister and best friend Jeannie. I cried by
myself against the side of the portable classroom at recess
every day for months, feeling shipwrecked. My older sisters
were no help, lost in the crowded schoolyard, playing with
their friends.

"Gail cried again today," Glenna would announce at the
dinner table, and my mother's features would fall.

I knew my sisters thought I was weak, but I was terrified
that my mother might too. I soon discovered that I could

mitigate the pain of our separation and her disappointment in me by being a good student. School work became my salvation.

✢

My First Communion was a momentous experience, an initiation into the church ritual that was the climax of every Catholic Mass. My white communion dress had a fitted bodice and a wide skirt with a crinoline, a hand-me-down from my older sisters. But my knee socks were new and felt like silk, and I wore newly polished white shoes, white gloves and a white veil. I could barely suppress my excitement. I would be receiving the host every week now, and the host was nothing less than the body of Christ. I looked at myself in the bathroom mirror and realized something else. Even at six years old, I could rock a veil.

My mother took many photographs of me before we left for the service. In the living room against the drapes, in the backyard against the trees, and on the front driveway. I had the same expression in every one. She was very pleased when the pictures were developed. I'd held my hands flat together at chest height, fingers pointing heavenward in prayer, with my eyes settled gently on the camera, solemn and serene. She commented on how pious I looked compared to Linda and Glenna in their First Communion photos, and my heart leapt at her approval. Linda beamed with excitement and pride in her photos, while Glenna looked uneasy.

I, however, had been serious and subdued and beatific, like the Virgin Mary herself.

One day, my mother told me a story that stuck in my memory like barbed wire. When she and my father first came up to Toronto from Prince Edward Island, they rented a room from a lady with a thick accent. Because my mother was only eighteen years old and had lost her own mother at the age of eight, this landlady took an interest in her and treated her with maternal kindness. She was Jewish, my mother said, which seemed to me an exotic thing. During the Second World War, in the landlady's home village, the Nazis locked all of the local Jewish children in a small schoolhouse and set the building on fire. The children screamed at the windows, their hair in flames, their faces melting, their helpless and hysterical parents forced to witness their children's agonizing deaths. The images haunted me at night.

I wanted very badly to be a hero. But I didn't feel heroic. I had already survived death, but rather than making me feel tough, my birth story seemed to have the opposite effect. Having died once, I only found the thought of my next death more frightening still. And though I wasn't always fearful, and could easily climb the pear trees in our backyard and ride my bicycle with no hands, I felt small and vulnerable on the inside.

Except in my sleep. I began to have recurring dreams in which I saved children from certain death. "Quick, this way!" and I would lead them all to safety, climbing over broken furniture and crumbling walls, flames in the background. Interestingly, in these dreams I was always a handsome young man with dark hair, like my dad. The only heroes I had ever seen were on TV, and they were all male. As much as I loved Saint Bernadette, she was sickly and weak. I couldn't imagine her saving anyone's life. I sought a role model for female "heroism" in the church, but could only find the stoically suffering Mother Mary and a chorus of martyred saints. I tried to picture myself growing up to be a tall and powerful nun, striding down a convent corridor in a long black gown with a stiff white rim of fabric around my face. It was the only sort of female caped crusader I could imagine.

✤

I had been going to school for a few months when I arrived home one day to find my mother in front of the TV set, pale and stiff. She told me that the Russians—the godless people of whom I was already so afraid—wanted to put missiles on an island near the United States named Cuba, from which they could easily aim and shoot missiles at us. She didn't have to spell out the consequences. I could see our house catching fire, my family trapped inside like the Jewish children in Nazi Germany.

But President Kennedy stood up to the Russians, and within days, the Russians turned their boats full of missiles around and went home, back across the ocean. It was a miracle—a miracle, surely, because President Kennedy was a Catholic. With God on his side, President Kennedy had saved our lives.

⚓

Every month we went to confession, and every month I had to come up with some sins to confess. I confessed the same ones every time: "I disobeyed my parents" and "I fought with my sisters." They were my standbys, even when they weren't especially true. That meant I was sometimes lying about my sins, which was itself a sin. It wasn't that I thought I was without sin. I just didn't know how to put my sins into words—my cowardice, my fear of letting my mother down, my anxiety about being a martyr. Even in my early years of elementary school, I often felt a heavy weight, a profound sadness and disappointment in myself. But mundane sibling squabbles were the only sins I knew how to describe while kneeling in the confessional, so my real fears and anxieties went undisclosed.

⚓

On the very last day of grade one, my teacher asked me to stand in front of the class, where she presented me with a pale blue plastic clamshell. She started clapping, and the children around me joined in. The clamshell opened to reveal a tiny painted statue of the Virgin Mary with a beautiful crystal-blue rosary circling her feet—my reward for standing first in the class. I was taken by surprise, thrilled, but all I cared about was showing my mother. When I ran through the front door holding open my clamshell, the rosary dangling out, she was delighted, and I was so happy that she was happy. I decided to share something else I thought she would like. I had decided, I told her, that I was going to be a nun when I grew up. She laughed, but that evening she shared my desire with my father and older sisters, and later on with other relatives too.

⤸

The first time I saw my mother cry was when her father was diagnosed with cancer. The second time was when President Kennedy was assassinated. Even though President Kennedy was the first Catholic president ever, and the best president, even though he was a hero who had fought and beaten the Russians, he had been shot dead in his convertible car in the street, in front of everybody. Just like that.

My mother's emotional reaction, the breakdown of her normally stoic demeanour, was deeply unnerving. I stood beside her in the middle of the living room as she watched Walter Cronkite on the nightly news, and looked up to see her slack mouth, her eyes shining, tears on her cheeks. I tried to understand it. I couldn't believe that God would allow President Kennedy to be killed.

Now who would stop the Russians? *Now* who would save the world? Would God? Because God hadn't even saved President Kennedy. And if he hadn't saved President Kennedy, why in the world had he bothered to save *me*? Was there any amount of personal sacrifice that could possibly justify my second birth? Devoting my life to God was the only thing I could think of. It was the very least I could do.

7

PRAYER

I KNEW THAT MY VERY EXISTENCE WAS DIRECT PROOF of the power of my mother's prayers, but it wasn't until grade five that I experienced the power of my own. It came when I least expected it, at the worst time of my young life.

I was reserved at school. Especially at recess. Others talked to each other more than to me. I was lonely, but I also felt different, and I let that feeling put a distance between my classmates and me. One day, an extroverted girl suddenly took an interest in me. Cindy was a tomboy with shoulder-length dark hair and slightly aggressive self-confidence. She was tall for her age. I admired her nerve and her wild and careless grin, which stood in such contrast to my wariness. I imagined these qualities came from the fact that she had big brothers, and I envied her, thinking they must be more fun than big sisters. She already had a group of friends—who were almost more like followers—but for some mysterious reason, she wanted me to be her friend too. I hadn't had such a deliberate offering of friendship before, and I was cautiously flattered and grateful.

It didn't last long. Overnight, it seemed, Cindy changed her mind. She told me she didn't want to be my friend after all. I realized that she'd only thought she liked me until she got to know me better and saw past appearances to the real me. I was not the person she thought I was, and this revelation went right to the core of all of my anxiety. I was an imposter, a pretender, a fake. Most of all, I was a disappointment.

I became horribly intimidated by her. It was as if she knew a terrible secret about me, and I was at the mercy of her discretion. At recess, I would try to hide from her in the crowded schoolyard. I was sick with the fear that she would talk about me behind my back, and make others laugh at me. I had always worried that I was a crybaby, and now, at ten years old, I felt in constant danger of tearing up in front of other kids.

The next day, despite my attempts to avoid them, Cindy and her friends spied me at recess. I saw them from across the schoolyard, racing toward me, Cindy in the lead. It looked like they were going to run straight at me. I was cold with fear but unable to move my feet. I tried to look away. I tried to be invisible. But from the corner of my eye I could see them closing in. I braced myself for a horrible impact. At the last second, the girls veered, each giving me a dismissive little push on my upper arm as she flew by, one after the other in turn. Not enough to knock me over. It was the gesture that counted. It broke me.

I suffered the long walk home at the end of that day with tears streaming down my face, blurring my vision of the sidewalk. I felt sick to my stomach and hopelessly trapped. I was terrified that Cindy and her gang would catch up to me, would step into my path and confront me with my failings. Making matters worse, my weeping form caught the eye of Billy, an obnoxious boy from my class, who then followed me for blocks, taunting from behind. His tone swung between aggressive interrogation and cruel mockery. He wanted to know why I was crying, almost as if he cared. When I wouldn't tell him, it only made him hostile. For all my humiliation, I couldn't stop crying.

I didn't leave my bedroom that night, even for dinner. My mother stood at the door and demanded to know what had happened. I hid my face from her while I sobbed about Cindy. She stood at a distance from my bed. She seemed irritated. I knew she was angry with Cindy, but I feared she was also angry at me, at my cowardice, my timidity and my inability to stand up for myself.

Glenna came into the room and began pacing, demanding to know what was going on. It was hard for me to describe without making it sound insignificant. I wept. Glenna angrily vowed to take matters into her own hands. I was grateful to her, but I was also afraid. I was convinced that if Glenna confronted Cindy it would only make things worse, leading to fresh and harsher reprisals in the schoolyard. I imagined a violent escalation of my persecution.

That night, I prayed to the Blessed Virgin Mary for help, believing she was my last hope. I said the Hail Mary over and over and over, each repetition more fervent than the last.

The next morning I woke feeling enervated. I had done all I could. My life was now entirely in her hands. I dragged my feet as I walked to school, arriving late. The bell had rung and the kids were all inside. I walked across the empty school-yard and slipped in through the school's big double doors. As I snuck past the principal's open door, I took a furtive peek inside. And that's when I saw Cindy. She was sitting, hunched over, across from the principal's desk. Her eyes were red. Her face was wet. She looked up and, for a moment, our eyes met. Then she looked away. I was stunned.

I entered my classroom to find my teacher missing. What luck! I scurried into my own chair. I could feel my classmates' excitement. Someone leaned in and told me what had happened. Cindy had been caught standing on top of the teacher's desk, attempting to move the second hand of the clock. A prank. The normally cheerful Mrs. Dorey had walked in, caught Cindy right in the act, and had become absolutely furious. Practically possessed. Now Cindy was in deep trouble in the principal's office.

I was awestruck. I was certain my prayers had somehow precipitated this miraculous turn of events and that Mrs. Dorey, with her completely out-of-character show of temper, had merely been God's instrument.

Cindy had been punished, but something else had happened too. The moment I had seen her in tears and vulnerable, I somehow knew she would never bully me again. And I was right. Cindy never apologized, but she kept her distance from that day forward. The ordeal was over.

On that morning in grade five, my prayers had been answered with a true miracle, and I felt enveloped in divine compassion. The Blessed Virgin Mary's intervention also quieted my slow-mounting anxiety that I was not the person I was supposed to be; it seemed to reaffirm the supernatural trajectory of my life. I felt such gratitude. And I felt so indebted.

8

COVETOUSNESS

IN 1967, MY FATHER LEFT HIS FACTORY JOB AND became the manager of his own gas and service station at the corner of Kipling and Evans Avenues on the southwest side of town. This was much more challenging than any job he'd had before; he was the boss now, with more pressure and responsibility and longer hours. The new job did bring in more money, which was fortunate, because five years after the birth of John, my mother was pregnant again. This would bring our total family size to nine, and our little North York bungalow wasn't going to cut it any more.

That summer, we moved into a brand new backsplit with five bedrooms, a fireplace in the family room and a large basement recreation room, located in the then-fledgling west-end suburb of Etobicoke. This was my mother's dream house. Within a few months of moving in, she gave birth for the eighth time, to a son named Jamie.

The service station business was good, and our house was soon filled with new furniture and decorated with textured wallpaper and Italian ceramic tiles. My parents bought a nine-piece cherry wood dining room set and a large crystal chandelier. My mother began collecting a beautiful and expensive china dinner set and crystal wine glasses. Gold-framed hall mirrors and a huge faux "old masters" framed painting of the Champs-Élysées replaced some of the religious iconography that had decorated our previous home.

Perhaps it was as much a reflection of my increasing inclination to worry, but it seemed to me that our improved finances and big new house had made my parents more tense and unhappy than before. My mother's daily life was certainly even more gruelling now. The bigger home, with larger rooms and more bathrooms, meant more space to clean, and with a new baby, there was now another mountain of cloth diapers to wash. My mother was thirty-six years old with seven children and no breaks.

During many of the years that followed, my father worked six long days every week. He went to bed early and left the house in the morning before anyone else got up. In the evening, he came home exhausted, smelling of gasoline and grease and cigarettes. He would eat by himself in the family room, hunched over his dinner plate, eyes on the TV evening news. He only joined us for supper at the kitchen table on Sundays.

On weekdays, my dad didn't touch a drop of booze. But on Saturday evenings he would come home dead-eyed with exhaustion, the beginnings of a weekend ritual already on his breath. Sunday soon became my least favourite day of the week. At Mass, he would sit in our pew looking sick and sour. During lunch, the tension would build as he went for his first beer of the day. The atmosphere of anger and resentment increased through the afternoon, as my dad sat in a solitary stupor, watching TV. It culminated at the supper table, when the evidence of my father's drinking was most glaring. We all tried to ignore it. Gradually, we children came to fill the air with loud banter, competing for attention, for distraction, while my parents ate in silence—my father in a sullen haze, my mother in a tense rage.

That Christmas, in grade six, I got my very first diary. It was green, and came with a tiny gold metal lock and key. Initially, I filled it with entries that read like reports: "Went to library" or "Watched hockey game." Later, I began to use full sentences like, "Mom and Dad fought all day over dad's drinking." Each Sunday evening, after my mother had washed and dried the dishes and my father had dragged himself off to bed, his alarm clock set for 6 a.m., she would sit on the upholstered rocker, her feet up on a matching ottoman in front of the TV, newspaper crossword on her lap, her face stony cold with fatigue and anger. I felt sorry for her.

Years later, my siblings Melanie and John began working at the gas station on Saturdays, and reported seeing a very different side of my father there. He laughed and chatted and joked with his brothers, who worked for him, and with his customers. I never saw this with my own eyes, and found it difficult to imagine.

⤙

I had now completed grade six at my new primary school, St. Marcellus Catholic School, and by the following summer was beginning to feel a little more at home there. I had just been invited to my first-ever birthday party. I was very nervous, worried about what I'd wear and if the present my mother had helped me pick out would be good enough.

The birthday girl, Patricia, had the longest, nicest hair in our class, and huge blue eyes. I arrived at the party to discover that her house was even bigger and fancier than ours. Her father was a successful businessman. He also played the piano and sang like a professional. All of the girls from my class gathered around him as he played, and in between songs, he told jokes and affectionately teased Patricia. He led us in a big, loud version of "Happy Birthday to You." It was in the middle of the song, with Patricia and her dad looking at each other, grinning, that a lump began to form in my throat. My eyes began to sting. Until that moment, I had believed that all fathers were depressed and disengaged by nature.

Had my dad and I ever even made eye contact? Had we *ever* just smiled at each other? Had he ever once asked me a casual question, expressed any curiosity or concern about my life? As everyone swayed to the music around the piano, singing and grinning, I fought back a bitter, choking, self-pitying pain as my eyes filled with tears.

Patricia blew out the twelve candles on her birthday cake and everyone cheered and clapped. I did too, keeping my eyes cast down until they finally began to clear. I realized how badly I wanted to be more like these girls. I wanted the life they had. I wanted to feel normal and happy. But I feared that God had other plans for me.

My father and me at my grade eleven
Father-Daughter Dance.

PART 2

9

CONFIRMATION

THE OTHER GAIL HAD BEEN A PERPETUAL BABY IN my mind, a beautiful angel, like baby Jesus in the manger. But that picture, frozen in the frame, was about to thaw.

The summer of 1968 found me on the cusp of my twelfth birthday, and hovering on the threshold of a change in body and soul. Linda and Glenna were now in high school, with active social lives and boyfriends. Melanie and John were young children, and Jamie was still a baby. I remained closest to Jeannie, but I was feeling less and less like a child myself, and the two-and-a-half-year age gap between us seemed more profound. I'd always been so keen to indoctrinate her that I'd barely noticed how well she could think for herself. That summer, when I began to pull away from her and spent more and more time alone, perhaps she was happy for some space. In the midst of my large family, a deep solitude took hold of me.

After one year at my new school, the other girls were friendly, but I still felt like an outsider. I began to spend lots of time alone in my bedroom reading, mostly nineteenth-century books recommended by my mother. My mother was particularly a fan of Charles Dickens, whose protagonists were pure, poor and orphaned. I read all of her favourites.

When I wasn't reading, I was taking long bicycle rides through the northwest end of the city—suburban neighbourhoods constructed on what had been farmland barely ten years before. I'd go into a trance, so preoccupied by my thoughts that I hardly paid attention to my surroundings.

In my isolation, I began to imagine the other Gail differently. I wondered what she might look like if, after she died, she'd kept aging in a parallel ethereal state, coexisting alongside me as a kind of blurred mirror reflection, an adolescent ghost. Since she was one year older, I imagined she'd be about one inch taller, but otherwise, we were, of course, identical.

The other Gail lived in my bedroom with me, under my bed. I imagined her lying in the dark looking up at the bedsprings and waiting for me to return when I was away from the house. She was invisible to everyone but me, but she stayed hidden anyway, just in case. She never spoke except with her eyes, which were expressive and empathetic. She needed me, and I wanted to take care of her, even if it was only make-believe.

When our fall and winter catalogues from Simpsons-Sears and Eaton's arrived in the mail, I scoured the children's section and wrote out my shopping list for the other Gail: stretch pants with foot straps, skirts with elastic waistbands and matching striped T-shirts. I thought a brand new wardrobe of coordinating separates, lovingly chosen, might lift her spirits.

I never confided in anyone that I imagined the other Gail in this way—she was my little secret. For the first time in my life, she was a source of comfort and connection to me instead of an unattainable angelic ideal. Glenna might well think I was weak, but the other Gail who lived under my bed was even weaker. She was solely dependent on me. I, on the other hand, was living the life originally meant for her. I owed it to her to take care of her. I was her guardian angel.

Perhaps the other Gail's new identity was an expression of my loneliness, but her ghostly appearance in my life also revealed a dramatic shift in my own identity. It seemed I had stopped thinking of us simply as the same person with the same soul—she being me before the car accident, and me being her after. Now there were two of us, together, sharing the same moment in time, though living in different dimensions. But despite the obvious contradictions, I still held fast to my mother's story that I was the other Gail reborn. I still believed that I had to prove myself worthy in God's eyes for having been brought back to life. I didn't feel any less subject to the supernatural forces at play in the world. And, most importantly, having the other Gail under my bed didn't make me any less anxious about what my mother thought of me.

One day a few weeks before my twelfth birthday, my mother's stomach began to hurt. She shuffled slowly through some morning chores, then spent most of the day in bed. This behaviour was unrecognizable to her children.

Early the next morning, Linda, Glenna, Jeannie and I stood at the kitchen door and watched with dread as she came down the stairs a step at a time, pausing, holding her breath. She was fully dressed to go out, her grey eyes unfocused, her pale face stiff from the intensity of the pain. My father was at her side, holding onto her elbow. The descent took forever. When she finally got to the bottom step, we followed at her heels, terrified, as she shuffled along the hall to the front door. My father helped her outside and down the porch steps to the car.

Hours later, he phoned and told us she was having emergency surgery. They were going to take out her appendix. For the next four days while she was kept in the hospital, I prayed fervently to the Blessed Virgin Mary for her recovery. If she answered my prayers, I vowed to start attending Mass every day to show my gratitude.

Throughout the rest of that summer, I rode my bicycle to church every single morning to attend Mass. I sat alone in a pew in the vast, nearly empty church. There was only ever a handful of other people there, most of them middle-aged women. I listened to the priest's every word and watched his every gesture. I took communion every day. The pale, paper-thin wafer, the body of Christ, stuck to the roof of my mouth. The trick was to work it off with your tongue and swallow it without parting your lips. These familiar religious rituals gave me tremendous comfort.

One day, I was sitting in the second row, the closest I'd ever been to the very front—the organist to my left, the altar to my right. I felt enveloped by a mystical calm, as if I were gently floating, carried on a breeze that cooled the back of my head. Suddenly, I was looking up only inches from the sour face of the organist. I could feel the cold wooden pew against my cheek. The organist pulled me upright with a firm grip—I had lost consciousness. I sat up, weak and disoriented. When the Mass was over she walked by me with a smirk on her face, saying I should eat more breakfast in the morning.

I never discussed my decision to go to church on weekdays with anyone, and no one at home, including my mother, ever asked why I was doing it. But my mother was fully aware that when I hopped on my bike every morning, I was heading off to church. And I could tell that she approved. It was looking more and more like I was going to be a nun after all.

I was now old enough to babysit, and I began to enjoy taking care of Jamie. As he fussed in his crib, I'd gently pat him on the back and sing lullabies until he stopped crying and fell asleep. I liked to pretend that the touch of my hand on his back worked like magic. I could almost feel the power pass through me to him, dissolving his distress. In my daydreams, I sometimes imagined myself healing the sick just by touching them, long lineups forming on a sandy beach somewhere in the Holy Land. I pictured the gratitude of the mothers whose children I had saved moving me to tears.

⌇

That fall, after I'd started grade seven, I made my sacrament of confirmation. Now there would only be two sacraments left in my life: either the sacrament of marriage or holy orders, depending on whether I got married or took my vows to become a nun, and extreme unction, or last rites, on my death bed. I knew that holy orders wasn't a decision that would be left up to me alone. One had to receive a calling from God. I wasn't sure whether I'd been called yet or not. But just in case, I began saying the rosary in my bed at night. I wanted to be ready. I wanted to be worthy. I wanted to be pure.

Around the time of my confirmation, I received my first holy scapular. Scapulars are made of cloth, with brown felt squares the size of large postage stamps attached on opposite ends of a loop of string. They are worn over the head like a yoke, with one square hanging down on the chest and the other between the shoulder blades, and always underneath your clothes. On one square of my scapular was an image of the Virgin Mary making her miraculous appearance as Our

Lady of Mount Carmel in 1251. On the other square was the promise she made to witnesses on that day: "Whosoever dies wearing this scapular shall not suffer eternal fire."

This promise seemed monumental to me. Simply by wearing a scapular even a sinner could get into heaven. Now *that* was magic.

⤙

When I was years younger, before I knew anything about sex, I once overheard my mother discussing the fate of an unmarried woman who'd had a baby. I didn't understand how it had happened, only that she was humiliated. Her shame weighed heavily on my mind. Eventually, I sought out my mother, tears in my eyes. "I don't want to have a baby without being married," I cried. I imagined that the baby was a punishment from God, because I knew all babies came from him. She reassured me that God hadn't caused the woman's pregnancy. She had brought this situation upon herself.

I only learned how the woman had done this in grade seven. My classmates were discussing dirty song lyrics, and someone cited "let it out and let it in" from the Beatles' "Hey Jude" as being extra dirty. I asked why, and a classmate casually explained the mystery of romantic love and the miracle of procreation in one brief anatomical description. It sounded like the most embarrassing and awkward procedure imaginable, largely because I immediately assumed it was executed while standing up straight, face to face, and struggling to keep one's balance.

It is impossible to exaggerate the anxiety around sexuality in orthodox Catholicism. The church never explained what was inherently bad about sex. They left that to the imagination. But it is no accident that the Catholic Church's most common moniker for Mary, "the Blessed Virgin," celebrates her sexual abstinence.

According to traditional Catholic faith, Mary remained a virgin her entire life, even during her marriage to Joseph the carpenter. That's how pure and holy she was. The church allowed sex within marriage among ordinary people, but only because it could lead to pregnancy. Any sex that interfered with God's gift of procreation was sinful. Mary's simultaneous embrace of both motherhood and virginity might seem to non-Catholics like a murky message, but the prohibition against sex outside marriage was crystal clear. It was a mortal sin, a sin of the very worst kind. Mortal sins on your soul could send you straight to hell.

⤙

In the fall of that year, on a lazy Saturday afternoon, I went for a bike ride that cut through the St. Marcellus schoolyard. There were several boys and girls my age standing and talking near the entrance. I recognized a girl from school, and she waved and greeted me. When I stopped the bike, she asked if I lived nearby. A boy who was listening said he lived a block up the same street, beyond a small cul-de-sac that was right across from my house. He had a pleasant smile, and I liked his collar-length brown hair. I mentioned I was babysitting at a house on that cul-de-sac that very evening. We chatted a little longer, and as I was leaving, the boy said he might drop by while I was there, just to say hi. He knew the house. I was caught off guard, but he seemed polite and I didn't want to be rude. I said okay.

That evening, sometime after the two little Debono girls had been tucked into their beds, I heard a light knock at the side entrance. I opened the door a few inches. The sun was already setting. The boy was standing in the shadow between the houses. Nervous, I stepped halfway out and we chatted shyly, awkwardly, in the dim light for less than a minute before my mother suddenly appeared on the sidewalk in a streetlight halo. She was heading toward us, carrying a large banana split ice cream dessert in a plastic container shaped like a boat. The family had gone to the local Dairy Queen for a Saturday night treat and she'd brought one back for me, a rare surprise.

When she caught sight of the boy, she stopped dead. The look on her face was petrifying. I understood it in an instant—disgust. I had abandoned my sacred post as guardian of the innocent sleeping children to indulge in some vain and licentious interaction with an unscrupulous boy. Then she jerked forward and contemptuously held out the banana split. She wouldn't even look at me. I took it with a barely audible "thank you," my heart pounding. She turned on her heel and was gone, back across the street. The boy, no doubt chilled to the bone, took off without so much as a goodbye. I never saw him again.

I shut the door and locked it, and walked on weakened legs up the side stairs to the kitchen. I thought I might pass out from sheer dread. I had never seen my mother look so angry with me before. I began racing through a stream of defences: I had not invited him. He had just shown up. I would never, ever have let him into the house. I hardly knew him. I don't have a boyfriend. I don't want a boyfriend!

I was so sick with fear I couldn't eat the melting ice cream. I sat fretting for hours until the Debonos came home. By that time my own house was in darkness, everyone asleep. I went to bed, full of foreboding.

The next day was a Sunday, and I stayed in my room until it was time to leave for Mass. As we squeezed into the family car to drive to the church, the tension was palpable. My mother still wouldn't look at me, and she continued to ignore me once we returned home. While everyone else ate lunch, I shut myself in my bedroom. When I thought it was safe, I snuck to the kitchen to make myself a peanut butter sandwich, but instead, I found my mother alone, drying dishes at the sink. I jumped slightly when I saw her. She bristled.

"I'm not surprised you're ashamed to show your face," she said.

"I didn't even know that guy," I blurted out.

She smirked, and continued drying the dishes with aggressive wipes.

"I only met him yesterday."

She didn't respond so I rushed on, my self-righteousness gaining momentum.

"He just dropped by that very second before you arrived because he heard me mention in the schoolyard that I was babysitting there last night and he lives nearby or something." I spoke of him now with contempt. "I don't know where he lives. I don't even know his name."

I thought I could detect a slight release of tension. I was making progress.

"And I had only just come to the door to see who it was and I would never have opened it wider or gone outside. Or let him in," I thought to add.

I drew strength from my impression that I sounded convincingly innocent. And despite having found him cute, I was now more than ready to throw his body on a pyre.

By suppertime, my mother had more or less settled down and stopped emanating anger. But her "guilty until proven innocent" attitude was a terrifying revelation that left me very anxious. I thought of the other Gail, a pure and perfect soul, lying under my bed. She had it easy. She would never know temptation. She would never need a scapular.

10

TEMPTATION

ON A HOT JUNE AFTERNOON IN THE LAST DAYS OF
grade seven, several of the girls in my class stood in the
schoolyard, their bare arms held high above their heads,
and amused themselves by comparing early signs of under-
arm hair growth. I lifted an arm up to show that I didn't
have any yet, but Kathy quickly corrected me, pointing to
fine strands of hair I'd never noticed before. It was as though
they'd suddenly appeared that very day, and I was shocked
to see them.

I was entering puberty, and by the end of that summer I
had turned thirteen and undergone a dramatic breakthrough.
Over just a few months, I had developed an emotional connection with other girls in my class, a feeling of shared identity and experience and interests. The other Gail, who had
been hiding under my bed for some time, was pushed to the

very back of my mind, replaced by flesh-and-blood friends, a core group of seven or eight who had collectively won my heart.

For the first time in my life, I found a little tribe outside of my family who knew nothing about my miraculous birth, who simply accepted me as one of them. I began to hang out with these girls after school and on weekends. We would tie up the phone for hours. I got louder, more expressive, more opinionated. I grew to care so much about my friends, and fitting in with them, that I began to care a little less about what my mother was thinking. I didn't need to behave better than them, or compete with them for approval—God's or my mother's. What we talked about most were boys.

My thirteenth year was the happiest of my life. My friends introduced me to a world view that stood in stark opposition to my mother's, where my interest in boys seemed normal. When my friends and I went to the mall, we spent our time on the lookout for cute boys our age. We might even strike up a conversation with them, and then reminisce about it for days afterwards. One day, I even confessed to a friend that I thought it would be a shame to die a virgin. When I heard the words come out of my mouth, I immediately felt guilty, as if I'd been caught showing off. We all knew that sex before marriage was a sin, but unlike me, my girlfriends weren't expecting God's call to become a nun.

I sometimes felt conflicted. I worried that I wasn't as good and pure as I used to be. I feared that something inside me, *someone* inside me, was getting lost. But I also felt more excitement and optimism than I could ever remember.

On January 1, 1970, I wrote in my diary: *New Year's Resolution: have confidence, be natural, be strong.*

That pubescent swagger was short-lived. As soon as I entered the all-girls St. Joseph Islington High School in the fall of 1970, my bravado began to fizzle. My friends and I were scattered into different homeroom classes and soon they were forming new bonds. We were still friends, but I'd lost the security and familiarity of a small clique. I envied the popular girls who bounced boldly down the halls between classes, and I feared the nuns, most of whom seemed distant and intimidating. None struck me as an advertisement for the cloistered life. I slowly reverted back to my former, more introspective self.

I buried my solitude in sewing, an intense, obsessive hobby I took up that year. It consumed all of my spare time. I spent every cent of my babysitting money in fabric stores. The act of sewing comforted me, distracted me and allowed me to hide. I would pass most of my teenage home life alone in my bedroom, hunched over tissue patterns laid out over fabric on my bedroom floor, lost in the hum of the sewing machine and pop music on my transistor radio.

꒷

When I was fifteen, I went to my first high school dance, a social event held jointly with the all-boys high school nearby.

I had asked my mother and knew right away she wasn't happy about it, but she barely responded. I told her a few of my friends from St. Marcellus would be there.

I was standing against the wall of the gymnasium when a red-haired boy approached me and asked me to dance. We danced through several songs, standing awkwardly during the pause between each one. Then, after we'd talked for a bit, he asked me if I'd go out on a date with him. He seemed eager.

Patrick was a grade ahead of me, and on his high school's senior wrestling team. I wasn't sure I wanted to go out with him, but it felt awkward to say no. I told him I'd have to speak to my mother first.

I woke the following day to find her in a steely mood. It took me most of the afternoon to work up the nerve to ask. When I was ready, I found her in the kitchen, peeling potatoes for dinner.

"I met a guy at the dance last night," I said, trying to sound nonchalant.

She immediately let out a very unnerving guffaw. I took a breath and pushed on.

"Anyway, he wants to know if we can go out together sometime. On a date."

She didn't actually say "no." Instead, she wielded her paring knife over the potatoes with such agitation, rotating them with clenched fingers, I thought she'd cut herself.

I hadn't experienced this degree of hostility from her since the banana split incident a few years earlier. I was sure she hadn't been this angry with Linda and Glenna when they first began dating. I was suddenly overcome by a strong rush of resentment, a conviction that she was treating me differently. She was being unfair.

"Everybody I know goes on dates," I said. I dropped the names of old friends she knew. "Pat and Sandra have. He only wants to see a movie. It's a western."

"Who is this guy? You just met him. You don't know anything about him."

"He's just a normal guy. He's a Michael Power student. He's on a sports team. I think his father might be a doctor."

"So he's some big shot who thinks he can do whatever he wants? And I suppose he drives a car?"

"He didn't act like a big shot." That wasn't entirely true.

The more defensive and self-righteous I was, the more sarcastic and snide her responses became.

"And how do you know he doesn't go drinking with his friends? How do you know he doesn't take girls out just to park in a dark alley somewhere?"

"I don't know. He doesn't seem that way. He seems pretty mature."

She laughed with disdain again. "He seems mature? Wouldn't you like to believe that!"

I was outraged. What had I done to deserve such suspicion? Why didn't she trust me?

Despite my mother's objections, or perhaps because of them, Patrick became my first official boyfriend. We dated for about a month, driving around in his car, going to movies and burger joints. Every time we kissed, I was incredibly tense. He asked me why I was so "rigid." I asked myself the same question, and worried that something was wrong with me. One evening he locked me in a few wrestling holds to show off his skill. I was embarrassed and a little irritated. I realized he wasn't growing on me.

All throughout that month, I simply endured the seething disapproval of my mother. Her stony face, her stiff shoulders, the set of her jaw, all screamed barely suppressed rage. It was as though she was watching something intolerable unfold and was unable to stop it. She could barely stand to look at me. It wasn't until I broke up with Patrick that I felt some of her anger let up. The experience had completely shaken my confidence in her regard for me.

That summer, when I turned sixteen, I began experiencing waves of inexplicable depression. It was different from any sadness I'd ever felt before—not just an absence of happiness, not an emptiness or loneliness, but an overbearing, aggressive and intrusive presence. I knew that I had to fight it, or at least to hide it. I didn't want others to notice that something was wrong with me. I wanted to be normal, to fit in. I worked harder at engaging my friends. I found that lively conversation was a great cover. I was learning how to appear happy, how to hide the real me.

The following September, my all-girls school merged with the all-boys high school next door. The most immediate effect was that the girls' kilts got shorter. I took up my hem too. Some of the bolder girls also started to leave the second button from the top of their yellow blouses undone. The girls with breasts and good posture. I was a little envious, knowing the boys would like them best. I continued to fight and hide my regular fits of depression.

I had been on a couple of first dates with boys I couldn't relate to, and they weren't worth the grief I was given for them at home. Everything changed in November 1972, during fall exam week, when two boys struck up a conversation with my friend Cathy and me in the hallway. It turned out that one of them had had his eye on me for a while, or perhaps more accurately, on the back of my short kilt as he walked behind me in the crowded school halls. Before I'd ever seen his face, Angelo was, apparently, already smitten.

Angelo was a recent transfer from the public school system, and he didn't feel at home at our school. He was an outsider, surrounded by kids he didn't know. He was also cute, a northern Italian with green eyes and light brown hair. He was naturally athletic and could play almost any sport well, but he competed at the national level in track and field. The year before, he had briefly held the national record for the hundred-yard dash in his age group. At sixteen years old, he was unusually focused and self-disciplined.

We began to date, and I soon found myself overwhelmed.

I had never been the object of such overt affection before. I hadn't known what it was like to be hugged and caressed. He showered me with compliments and terms of endearment. Two weeks into our relationship, he told me he loved me. These words were utterly foreign to me—my parents had never said them—and they sounded extreme to my ears. I told him they made me uncomfortable, but he was unapologetic. He assured me that he fully intended to win over my heart. I went home that day with a stomach ache, full of anxiety, feeling powerless in the face of his passion.

Predictably, my new relationship with Angelo created enormous tension at home, and within a few weeks, it had built to an intolerable level. My normal interactions with my mother broke down completely, reduced to terse monosyllables spoken without eye contact. Every few days she would level a new verbal attack at me. She constantly repeated that she wanted Angelo and me to "cool it." I couldn't understand why she was so agitated and hostile. It felt as if the special status I'd always had with her had been turned on its head. Now she hated me.

Where once I would have been devastated to lose her approval, now I felt resentful. She was the one acting abnormal, not me. I wasn't doing anything wrong. And because of this, her anger was having the opposite effect to the one she'd intended. Faced with the divergent intensities of my mother's anger and Angelo's infatuation, Angelo began to feel more and more like my salvation. I drew closer to him, fearful my mother would try to pull us apart. We were partners in crime.

We were barely sixteen years old, but within six weeks of dating, Angelo was already talking about marriage.

My mother tried to enforce restrictions. She insisted I could only go out alone on a date one evening a week. We went to drive-ins and watched Bruce Lee kung-fu movies and Clint Eastwood westerns. But home visits were allowed. On other nights, Angelo and I stayed in, watching hockey games in the basement. He had little desire to hang out with anyone but me. Consequently, our social life narrowed right down to the two of us. We were soon spending all of our free time alone together, and much of that time was spent kissing after everyone else had gone to bed.

During one particularly passionate episode, I pulled away, and when Angelo asked if something was wrong, I began to cry. I confessed that maybe we *were* getting too serious and wondered if we should start to cool it after all. He asked why, but I was reluctant to say more. He wouldn't let up, so I finally confessed that I was afraid that if we kept up this pace, we were bound to "go all the way." I didn't want to lose my virginity. I was also afraid of the desire I felt for Angelo. I had become more modern, less judgmental about sex, but I was still terrified of committing such a grievous sin against the church.

Angelo didn't seem to suffer the same anxiety, but he expressed sympathy for my fears and reassured me that he would never try to have sex with me if I didn't want to. I was relieved to hear it, and grateful to know that even if we didn't have sex, he would still love me.

INTEMPERANCE

EVERY YEAR, MY SCHOOL HELD A FORMAL FATHER-
Daughter Dance in the gymnasium. In grade ten, my friends
had all attended, dressed in formal gowns, their fathers in
sharp suits. The dads got on well and the girls all hung
out together and everyone laughed and danced and had a
great time. I was left out, but that was okay. It just wasn't
something I could ever imagine doing with my father. We
barely spoke at home, and the idea of spending all evening
together away from the rest of our family seemed unimaginable to me.

So in grade eleven, when tickets for the dance went on sale
again, I said nothing about it. It was my mother who casually
suggested that I ask my dad to attend with me. I was shocked.
There had been so much tension between my mother and me
because of Angelo—we were barely speaking—and suddenly

this? What was she up to? I wondered if she was embarrassed that I would be the only one of my friends not going for the second year in a row. Did she feel bad for me? One thing I did know: there was no way in the world my father would want to go to this dance. He would hate the very thought of it. But after my mother pushed me to ask him again, I finally got up the nerve. It wasn't easy; we so rarely talked to each other. But when I asked him, he nodded, as if already resigned. I realized my mother had gotten to him first.

My friends' fathers were all successful businessmen. One was a lawyer. Another ran an insurance company. They were active in the community and volunteered as ushers at the church. My father was a shy Maritimer who worked with his hands. Even though he knew car engines inside out, and could add up long numbers in his head, he had only a grade school education. He wasn't going to fit in.

My mother was determined to make it happen. She bought my corsage and his carnation. She saw us off at the front door, smiling nervously. We were invited to my girlfriend Shelagh's house first for a cocktail hour. I left my dad down in the basement having drinks with the other fathers while I escaped upstairs to where my girlfriends were drinking pop and gossiping and laughing. But not before someone snapped a photo of us. In it, though the night was young, his face was already flushed.

That was the last time I saw my father for hours. I was shuffled out of the house and brought to the dance in another car. When we arrived at the school auditorium, there was a DJ playing pop music. People were milling around and dancing, but I couldn't find my dad anywhere. After a while, one of the other fathers came looking for me. He said my dad hadn't been feeling very well and was just resting a bit in the parking lot. There was nothing to worry about. But I knew why my father was sick.

I spent the rest of the evening by myself, leaning against the wall or sitting on a bench, occasionally chatting with friends. As time passed, I grew increasingly worried. No one asked me where my dad was. I feared it was because everyone already knew. I pretended that nothing was wrong, but on the inside, I was seething with embarrassment and anger.

After the dance, our group went off for a midnight snack at the Skyline Hotel on the airport strip. I saw my dad there, though we didn't sit together. He seemed sheepish, red-faced and haggard, but a little recovered. The other dads were kind to him. At the end of the evening, Shelagh announced she was going to drive me home herself. She said someone else would be driving my dad home in his car. She said this casually, cheerfully, trying to sound as though it was perfectly normal that my dad couldn't drive his own car home.

When I got home, I tiptoed up the stairs to my bedroom and quietly shut the door. My father was already home. Just as I was getting into bed, I heard my mother go down into the kitchen. I knew she'd come out to see me. I held my breath and listened, wondering if she would knock on my door. She knew what had happened—I could feel her fury blasting like a dragon exhaling fire through the house.

Eventually, I heard her turn off the kitchen light, then slowly climb the stairs and return to her bedroom. I started to feel sorry for her. I could imagine her mortification at the thought of my father making such a spectacle of himself in front of my girlfriends and their fathers. But I feared she was going to make it hell around the house, and that made me feel sorry for my dad too. We would all suffer.

There followed a few horrible days of icy silence and unbearable tension. I kept out of the way, hiding in my bedroom, sewing.

Early the following week, when no one else was around, my mother finally spoke up about what had happened. She got right to the point, but her voice contained a sadness I'd rarely heard.

"Your father drank too much at the dance because he felt so nervous around the other fathers and he was trying to relax."

I realized she was trying to explain his behaviour in an effort to forgive him, and to win my forgiveness for him too. I knew she was right, that he was naturally shy and had been intimidated by my friends' fathers, that he lacked self-confidence around them, and that he'd felt forced to go to the dance in the first place. I realized she was trying to stand by him, and she wanted me to stand by him with her.

He would never say anything to me about that evening, and he would never apologize. I never spoke of it again with my mother, siblings or friends. We all pretended it just didn't happen, and my father and I went on avoiding each other. But the experience revealed a hidden side to my mother, a deep heartache I'd never fully appreciated.

12

FORNICATION

IT TOOK ANGELO ABOUT SIX MONTHS TO WEAR DOWN my resistance to his sexual advances. I don't think he was making a conscious effort. I don't think he was thinking at all. Piece by piece of clothing, inch by inch of flesh, we progressed, and in May, we had sex in the front seat of his car, parked only a block from my house. We were still sixteen.

The next morning, I lied and told my mother we'd seen a movie the night before, a science fiction film starring Charlton Heston called *Soylent Green*. I was relieved that she didn't ask me about it, because other than having something to do with cannibalism, I didn't know anything. Instead, she was deadly silent. I casually added that it hadn't been a very good movie. A banal, gratuitous lie to cover up a monumental mortal sin.

In one way, I didn't feel all that different after losing my virginity. We'd been coming close for a while, and our first attempt was over in a flash. But something *had* changed. Something irrevocable. I had stepped across a dark divide, looking back at the angels and saints and the Blessed Virgin Mary from the wrong side. I was no longer pure and innocent. Once it was too late, the new experience I had gained seemed insubstantial compared to the inexperience I had lost.

But virginity wasn't something you could ever get back, and there didn't seem to be anything left to lose. Torn between guilt and rebellion, I convinced myself that it wasn't so sinful to have premarital sex, provided it was only with my future husband. It simply meant we would eventually have to get married, no matter what, to save our souls. I reconciled myself to this new stage in our relationship with considerable abandon, once the rest of the family had gone off to bed each Saturday night.

The risks we took were shocking. We were caught in compromising situations, once by Angelo's mother, and once by a policeman checking out parked cars in a park. But we were never caught in the act by my mother. More than that, since using dependable birth control would only have compounded our guilt in the eyes of the church, we used the rhythm method instead, which the church permitted for married couples. In addition to risking being caught, we were playing a monthly game of Russian roulette with our fertility.

One evening, Angelo picked me up at the fabric store where I had a part-time job after school. Before taking me home, he parked the car a block from my house so we could kiss good-night. My mother, thinking I'd be taking the bus late in the evening, had decided to pick me up from work herself with-out telling me. By the time she'd arrived at the fabric store, I had already left, and on her way home, she spied Angelo's parked car and the action going on inside. When I arrived home, minutes after her, she was standing in the hallway, head leaning forward like she was going to gag, choking on her disgust.

"And to think *we* thought *you* were going to be a *nun!*"

She spit the words at me and they penetrated like knives. I was overwhelmed by my feelings of resentment, grief and a despair I couldn't name.

My mother's extreme disappointment was devastating. I felt I had finally, fatally lost all value in her eyes, the special place I had held in her heart from birth. And inside me, where the other Gail had once nourished me, there was now only empti-ness. It was if she too recoiled at my shamefulness.

⤙

By the end of that summer, when I was about to enter grade twelve, I began having doubts about my intense emotional relationship with Angelo. I'd slowly become alienated from my girlfriends and I missed them. They were busy having just the kind of fun teenagers have: double-dating, going to parties and starting to drink alcohol socially too. Angelo and I never went to the popular local pub to socialize, and we never went to parties. With us, everything was serious and sober. He wanted to spend all of his free time with me and me alone.

Ironically, Angelo had many characteristics that my mother valued highly. For a teenage boy in the early 1970s, he was conservative and traditional. He was a paragon of abstemious living. He didn't smoke and he didn't swear. Much like my mother, he feared that alcohol would lead to licentious behaviour. He rarely drank, and he was eager to see that I didn't either. He could be jealous and insecure, and threatened by the thought of me socializing with other boys. He was plagued by anxieties of his own, and I wasn't privy to them, any more than he was privy to mine.

Several times I ventured to raise my doubts about our relationship, but I soon backed off when I saw the pain it caused. And I reminded myself that we had, after all, an iron-clad bond. We were having sex, and if there was going to be any redemption for our souls, it would have to be through marriage. We were as good as married already.

I began to experience what I called in my diary "five-minute depressions." Several times a week, sometimes once a day. The sadness came in sudden, intense and crushing waves that would briefly knock me off my feet, and then I would pull myself together again. When a crash was over, I shook it off like ashes, and then I felt relatively normal again. What mattered most was that no one had noticed, and I still looked fine.

For the first time in my life, Sunday Mass was a joyless experience. It was as though I was hearing the liturgy with a newly tainted ear. I'd heard these same hymns all my life, sang them all my life, but suddenly I was finding the lyrics irritating, or just plain stupid. The more I thought about what they said, the more ludicrous and arcane they sounded.

Oh God of loveliness
Oh Lord of heaven above
How worthy to possess
My heart's devoted love

On one packed car ride home from church, I raised the subject for the first time.

"Why does God need to be told we love him all the time?"

No reaction. I pressed on, aiming my barbs at my mother.

"Why does he need so many compliments?"

She bristled at my disrespectful tone, but said nothing.

"Does he really *like* all that flattery and fawning attention?"

She pretended to ignore me, but she was hurt by my irreverence, I could tell. There was tension in her jaw; her mouth was pursed. No one else in the car spoke up. They didn't dare.

Soon, I began looking at her soap operas with a cynical eye.

"How can you stomach this sickening stuff?" I asked her of the characters and stories she'd been watching for nearly twenty years. "Everyone's immoral. They're all vain and mean and liars and adulterers. They're disgusting people." In my tone was the subtlest of suggestions that she got some vicarious enjoyment from their sins.

You think you are so morally superior, I thought to myself. *But you are not.*

13

MAGISTERIUM

IT HAD BEEN A LONG TIME SINCE I'D THOUGHT OF the other Gail as a ghost hiding under my bed. She had abandoned me during the worst hostilities with my mother. But now, she was about to re-emerge in my life in a newly empowered form.

In my grade twelve math class, I sat beside a boy named Matthew. We rarely spoke, until one day he noticed I was carrying a Tolkien paperback. He smiled disapprovingly. He thought The Chronicles of Narnia was a much better read. Matthew spoke formally, and seemed good-natured but intense. My curiosity was piqued. A few weeks later, I got *The Lion, the Witch and the Wardrobe* out of the library. C.S. Lewis's religious subtext took me straight back to the seductive Catholic magic of my childhood. The noble, loving and infinitely wise Aslan was an irresistible Christ figure. Through his self-sacrifice, good conquered evil and the world of Narnia was saved. The sense of redemption, forgiveness and gratitude in the final pages of the book was as sweet and nostalgic to me as a piece of Turkish delight. While my childhood enjoyment of the Mass had recently suffered a guilt-ridden blow, I was still Catholic to the core. C.S. Lewis hadn't captured my imagination the way Tolkien had, but he had moved me to tears in a way that Tolkien could not.

In the minutes before and after math class, Matthew and I discussed the symbols in the book. It became apparent to me that he was unusually committed to his Catholic faith, with a medieval sense of religious devotion, and that he wanted to share it with me. I read the rest of the books in the series, and Matthew lent me copies of other more theological books by Lewis. I was surprised at how much I enjoyed them. I liked Lewis's intellectual approach to religion, which was less about simple observance and more about ideas and principles, things I could reflect on, analyze and discuss.

Matthew was a lightning-fast talker—animated and quick to laugh. I'd never met a teenager with so much religious enthusiasm. He was in a league of his own. He seemed to be receiving an extensive parallel education in Catholic instruction at home, as though he was being groomed for an ecclesiastical career by some mysterious mentor with direct links to the Vatican. Other kids might have thought him a little odd, but by the end of the school year, I began to find his combination of religious conviction and intellectual energy captivating.

He also happened to be very handsome, tall and lanky with long jet-black hair and smiling Irish eyes.

Around this time, my war with my mother began to settle into a tense truce. However bitter her disappointment in me, her rage seemed spent. We were still distant with one another, but we'd stopped fighting. She appeared resigned to Angelo, and the rest of my family liked him. He was now pumping gas on weekends at my father's station, evolving into the perfect future son-in-law. I still had anxieties about our relationship, but I stifled them in favour of less conflict in my life.

I mentioned Matthew to my mother, telling her about how he was one of the top students in the school, and that he was known to be an extraordinarily devout Catholic. I told her he was a big fan of C.S. Lewis, and she nodded approvingly. I knew she would.

"He's the kind of guy you could easily imagine becoming a priest," I added. "Maybe even a bishop or a cardinal."

He would cut a fine figure in those flowing black robes, I thought to myself, somewhat lustfully.

⊁

During this year, I graduated from writing in a daily diary to keeping a journal. I thought of my journal entries as letters. Soon, I was beginning each new entry with "Dear Gail." I wasn't writing to myself. I was writing to the other Gail.

I started imagining her as a wise, celestial spirit, looking down on me from heaven and taking a compassionate interest in my life. I hoped that writing to her might give me some much-needed guidance and insight. I wanted to share my problems with her, to review them, break them down and analyze them. What would *she* do if she were *me*?

⤙

It was the fall of 1974, my last year in high school. Matthew, having spent his summer vacation working at a monastery in Quebec, returned to class with a dramatic new look. His collar-length hair was gone, and in its place was an army-standard buzz cut that emphasized his chiselled features. Now his appearance was even more unusual and striking, and he exuded a confidence and conviction beyond his eighteen years. We shared a spare class and hung out together. It was the only time we got to see each other, and we made the most of it, with lively discussions and debates. Angelo was unhappy about it, and let me know many times. I explained that Matthew and I had an interesting intellectual friendship—and that was all.

The deadlines to apply to college and university were approaching. Angelo was still primarily interested in sports, and applied for a four-year university degree in physical education. We decided that I would do a two-year college degree in early childhood education and then work and save money for two years so we could get married as soon as Angelo graduated. But I was secretly plagued by uncertainty about my future career. I received no advice from home. It seemed to me that if I wasn't going to be a nun, my mother wasn't interested in what I might choose to do instead.

A month after I applied to college, the night before the Christmas break, I dreamed that Angelo and I broke up. I was jolted awake by the painful fear that I was making a terrible mistake about my education. I rushed to school early that morning—the halls empty. I arrived breathless at the door of the guidance office and was relieved to find a counsellor inside.

I applied to university, and when I was asked about a major I instinctively said political science. I would even qualify for an entrance scholarship. That evening, when I told my mother about my sudden change of plans, I had the vague impression that she approved. If Angelo thought it was a setback in our marital schedule, he didn't complain. He was just looking forward to getting out of high school, and no doubt getting me away from Matthew.

Throughout the final months of high school, my friendship with Matthew became more charged. We whispered and laughed together in the library. We discussed human values and eternal truths, the nature of God, morality and faith, oblivious to the students around us. We wrestled through these topics with energy and enthusiasm, often disagreeing but always friendly.

I thought about him more and more when I was outside of school, the things he would say, the way he looked. In school, in the sea of students shuffling through the halls between classes, I kept a constant watch for his distinctive dark buzz cut. I knew the routes he took to classes, the places I was most likely to run into him. A chance meeting, his raised eyebrow, a quick grin—just seeing his face in a crowd could make my day.

On a beautiful afternoon in May, Matthew and I spent our study hour sitting with legs outstretched on the grass at the side of the school's football field. He told me he admired that I sewed my own clothes. He said he thought sewing was a particularly honourable activity for a young woman, sounding like a character from a Jane Austen novel. In response, I complained about how men had all the power in the church when women were just as capable. I already knew the orthodox explanation: because Jesus's twelve apostles were all men.

"In fact, in many ways, women are morally superior to men," Matthew said. "God asks less of women because they don't need to work as hard to earn a place in heaven."

He said that's why the church placed women on a pedestal. He added, somewhat shyly, that in his opinion, a pedestal was where I belonged too. I felt myself blush, but then fought back from feeling flattered by such a mixed blessing.

"That 'pedestal' is so that women will stay in one spot, where you can keep an eye on them and make sure they don't go anywhere. A pedestal is like a prison."

He laughed at that.

It suddenly occurred to me that Matthew might well assume I was still a virgin, although I hadn't been for nearly two years, and I began to obsess over the thought that I wasn't as pure and innocent as he probably thought I was. The heavy guilt of having lost my virginity and the fear that I was heading for an ordinary life and not the life of my childhood fantasies, whether out of cowardice or lack of conviction, was a private torment that now redoubled in intensity.

It all came down to sexuality. There was a reason Saint Bernadette didn't have a boyfriend. Sex and the sacred just didn't mix. At least they weren't supposed to in my religion. By getting sexually involved with Angelo, had I failed to fulfill the very purpose for which I was reborn? Who did I think I was, rejecting what might have been a higher calling from God?

I feared that I had taken a wrong turn and allowed myself to become someone I was never meant to be. But Matthew made me feel as though that person was still inside me somewhere, the person I felt I had abandoned and betrayed. Perhaps even a servant of God. His belief in me gave me new hope. I didn't dwell on the truly contradictory nature of my feelings for him.

One day, he announced that he had something for me. It was a brand new scapular. I read the inscription on the back with a feeling of deep nostalgia: "Whosoever dies wearing this scapular shall not suffer eternal fire." I had long ago lost my first scapular, but this one I intended to keep safe. I needed all the help I could get. I wondered whether by some miracle I could find my true path again. I began to sleep with a rosary under my pillow, as though it radiated an invisible blessing that would magically wash the sins from my soul and redeem me. I even began to daydream about taking Holy Orders again.

Dear Gail, Sometimes I wish I could turn back time. Is it too late for me?

✦

That nostalgia for my childhood dream of being a nun didn't last. When my York University acceptance package arrived, I read through a range of course descriptions that sounded so exhilarating to me that I left all fantasies of the convent life behind. I began to enthusiastically select my first-year classes. When I shared my selections with Matthew, he peered at me with a furrowed brow. He said he was worried that York would be a negative influence on me. It was a secular institution, after all, he said, emphasizing "secular" like it was a bad part of town. I wanted to take a humanities course titled Greek and Biblical Perspectives on the Human Condition, and he was especially unhappy about this. He thought it was dangerous to dabble in classical texts without the guidance and wisdom of proper Catholic instructors. I felt deflated. Surely by now I was capable of withstanding Protestants?

Matthew argued that I would be much better off attending the same private Catholic college in New England to which his parents were sending him. At Magdalen College, the curriculum was based on the education principles of Cardinal John Henry Newman, a nineteenth-century Catholic theologian. He showed me his course outlines. I much preferred my York University reading lists. I couldn't bring myself to tell Matthew that the only appealing thing about Magdalen College was that he would be there.

As graduation approached, I felt increasingly distraught about saying goodbye to Matthew. I had grown so attached to him, dependent on our friendship and on our deep discussions. Angelo was still my boyfriend, and despite Matthew, the rhythm of our relationship had stayed largely unchanged. We hung out every weekend and talked on the phone every night. I couldn't imagine ever breaking up with him. I continued to have an affection for him, and an attraction. But we didn't connect on an intellectual or spiritual level. Matthew was the only person in my life I felt I could truly relate to. I started having trouble eating and sleeping.

Matthew's mood changed too. He seemed increasingly introspective. One day, speaking more softly than usual, he told me he wished I could visit his parents' cottage over the summer. He said he could imagine sitting on the porch steps with me at night, looking up at the stars and holding hands. He said that would be his definition of pure happiness. I was astounded. It was the first time he had ever spoken so personally. Then, something like fear flashed across his face and he quickly assured me that holding hands was *all* he had been imagining.

That night I felt physically ill. When I tried to imagine just holding hands with Matthew under the stars at night, I knew I would want to kiss him. He would figure out quickly that I wasn't a virgin.

Soon afterwards, Matthew surprised me by asking if he could visit me at my home on a Saturday afternoon. I'd never seen him outside of school hours before. I was extremely apprehensive, and anxious that he might find my family or home somehow inferior.

I told my mother that Matthew—the devoutly Catholic friend I'd mentioned—would be visiting. She didn't ask questions, but that morning she baked a batch of cookies just for us, something she'd never done for me before. The cookies surprised me almost as much as Matthew's request to visit.

Matthew arrived at two o'clock sharp in a dark, well-fitted suit, looking strikingly handsome. My mother came to the door with me and I introduced her to him. When they shook hands, my mother's face lit up. He had perfect posture and impeccable manners. The three of us sat down in the living room on the French provincial couch and chatted politely. Matthew was effusive about my mother's cookies, and she smiled her self-conscious, slightly crooked smile. I saw his eyes drift briefly up to a crucifix above the living room entrance. I sensed his approval, and her approval too.

After a short while, my mother tactfully excused herself. Matthew relaxed, as though he'd just completed a job interview. We talked a little more, but it was small talk, something unfamiliar to us, and it felt awkward. He didn't stay much longer. I closed the front door behind him feeling vaguely disappointed. *What was that all about?* It had been an odd visit—friendly, but formal. It reminded me of another scene from a Jane Austen novel. Had Matthew come to check out my home, my mother ... our crucifixes? Had we passed some kind of test?

⤙

With only days left in the school year, my anguish over saying goodbye to Matthew grew steadily more acute. I wept in bed at night, hopelessly torn.

Dear Gail ... I can't see any way out. I can't break up with Angelo to go out with Matthew. That isn't even an option. It's totally hopeless. But how can I go on without seeing Matthew? All I can think about is blurting out my true feelings, even if it's the last time we ever speak.

Angelo and I had been dating for two and a half years. It felt like a marriage, even though we'd never spent a night together. I knew that breaking up now would be so destructive that it would feel like a divorce, and like premarital sex, divorce was a huge sin in the Catholic Church.

On the morning of the very last day of high school, a hot day in June, Matthew and I met in the hallway and, in a desperate whisper, I finally confessed my overwhelming grief at our imminent separation. I was choking back tears. Matthew's own face was flushed with distress. He quickly, nervously admitted he had also been asking himself what would happen to us. Then he ventured further.

"What if God meant us to be more than just friends?" he said. "What if he meant us to be together?"

We looked into each other's eyes. It felt as if the clock was ticking down and we only had hours left to save ourselves from a tragic ending.

Then Matthew suggested a plan: that we meet in the school chapel during our lunch hour and pray to God together, to ask for His guidance. He believed that God might give us a sign about our future, whether we should be together or apart. It took me by surprise, but I agreed to meet him. I felt hopeful that perhaps God would somehow intervene in our dilemma. But I was also terrified that, for Angelo, this chapel rendezvous would amount to infidelity. It might as well have been a motel room.

At noon, I slipped into the chapel, my heart pounding. It was empty except for Matthew, kneeling in a pew waiting for me. He looked nervous and excited. I knelt down in the pew that was across the aisle from him, close but just out of arm's reach, and we bowed our heads in parallel prayer. We didn't have to pray for long. God answered within minutes.

The chapel doors burst open with a bang and Angelo stood there, winded and red-faced. He was furious to have caught us alone together, as if a year of agonizing suspicions had been confirmed. Crushed, he stumbled backwards out of the chapel entrance in tears.

One look at his face and my whole body went cold with fear and shame. I jumped to my feet, leaving Matthew kneeling in his pew, and ran after Angelo. He raced ahead of me down the school hall, outside through the double doors, across the running track and through the football field. I chased after him the whole way, calling his name.

He was heading for the train tracks that ran just beyond the north boundary of the school, crying and calling out that if I was leaving him, he was going to kill himself. I struggled to keep up, crying myself now, begging him to stop. My horror at the possibility of causing his death had driven out every other thought. I swore that nothing had ever happened between Matthew and me, and that I wasn't breaking up with him. He finally stopped running and turned around. I doubled over in pain, pouring out assurances and frantic apologies between gasps for air.

"Matthew and I were only praying together because it was the last day of school! That's all it was."

Angelo finally calmed down. We walked east along the railway boundary, away from the school, weak-kneed and breathless. I didn't see Matthew again that day. We never said goodbye.

⤙

I began my summer vacation in a state of shock. I stayed shut up in my bedroom for days and only came out to pick at the food on my plate. I felt my mother's worried eyes on me but she never asked me what was wrong.

Then, about three days later, she handed me a letter that had just arrived in the mail. My name and address were written in a formal script with a fountain pen. The envelope was made of elegant paper, a pale antique yellow. Inside was a matching piece of paper folded in three and sealed with an *M* in real red sealing wax.

Dear Gail,
May you be truly happy for then I am happy too. I do miss
you but the will of God, which has manifested itself by our
separation, causes me to rejoice, for is not His will the best?
I hope I am still your good friend as you are mine.
Should you ever need me I remain,
Your willing servant,
Matthew

I felt myself choking with anger and disappointment. Did he really believe it was God's will that we be separated? Shouldn't God have more important things to do than get involved with us? For a brief moment, I'd hoped Matthew might declare his love for me and announce he was coming after me like a crusading knight, but his medieval formality and sense of resignation in the face of divine intervention only left me feeling hurt. I had been relinquished so easily. But I consoled myself that the situation had been hopeless from the start. Completely hopeless. I'd been terrified of revealing my sexual past. Now, at least, he would never need to know.

I was aware of my mother, anxiously hovering nearby as I read Matthew's letter. Hesitantly, I passed it to her. She read it, then handed it back, silently, with sorrowful eyes. I grabbed it and ran back upstairs to my bedroom to cry.

My parents and me at my graduation
from York University.

PART 3

14

REFORMATION

Dear Gail, I turned nineteen today.
Time to grow up. Time to move on.

⤙

The main campus of York University was 457 acres on the northern boundary of Toronto. It looked like a vast industrial park, a concrete outcrop in a barren landscape. It was broken up by giant parking lots and connected by narrow, serpentine roadways. As the days got shorter, the November air blasted in wind tunnels between the grey buildings. In the worst of winter, it felt like an Arctic military outpost. But after the heated melodrama and angst of my high school years, York's cold brutalist campus was fresh and bracing. It was just what I needed. It was something new.

The very first university paper I wrote was for a children's literature course, and I called it "Why There is No Juvenile Delinquency in Narnia." I painstakingly analyzed all of the Christian symbolism and themes in *The Lion, the Witch and the Wardrobe* and argued that, in the real world, these religious values are what give children a firm moral foundation in life. With less exposure to religion, young people are more likely to despair that life has no meaning, and therefore more likely to commit crimes or even commit suicide. I was very pleased with my essay. When my professor handed the papers back, she asked to speak with me after class. She had given me a B. She said she thought my paper was, in a sense, well written, but that I had made some gigantic assumptions about the dependence of morality on religion. I left the meeting feeling perplexed, and suspecting that she must have some personal hang-ups about God.

My second paper, for my political science course called An Introduction to Canadian Government, earned an A. There was something to be said for sticking to the facts.

That fall, Matthew and I exchanged letters wherein he continued to question my decision to attend a secular university. He quoted Aristotle, suggesting I should be studying universal truths before anything so specific as Canadian government. But what concerned him most was that I was going to be reading the Bible before getting a proper foundation in Catholic theology. That was dangerous, he thought. I was beginning to get testy. I didn't want to have to keep defending my academic choices. Why couldn't he just trust me? The more preachy he became, the more contrary was my response.

"Sorry to put you on the defence," he wrote, "but I'm somewhat puzzled at why you are urged to contradict me. I hope it's out of a quest for truth, for should you present a convincing argument for your education, I would seriously consider leaving here."

He would consider leaving Magdalen? Did he not believe wholeheartedly in his own choices? Should I be trying harder to get him to come home?

He continued, "I know that you don't want to come to Magdalen and there isn't anything I could say that would change your mind (perhaps). But I am concerned that perhaps you are not getting all that it takes to satisfy your love of knowledge."

His letters could be exhausting. I didn't want to be in a spiritual arm-wrestle with an aspiring priest who might or might not have his own hidden doubts. The playful spark between us was gone, and his tone seemed more and more formal with each letter. I longed to be in the same room with him again, if only so I could smack him. Besides, I was done with having my life feel like a soap opera. I wanted to focus on my education, and that meant I needed my emotions to settle down.

What Matthew didn't appreciate was how intellectually engaging I found my university classes. In my humanities course, Greek and Biblical Perspectives on the Human

Condition, my tutorial leader gently prodded us with deep and sometimes personal questions about big ideas—truth, goodness, justice and love, and challenged us to think beyond black and white answers. My catechism wasn't much help to me now. I had to try to put my thoughts into my own words.

In that same course, I also learned not to call the Hebrew Bible the "Old Testament" because that's a Christian name that implies that Jesus was the Jewish Messiah who made everything "new" again. But unlike Christians, Jews are still waiting for their Messiah. This was a seismic shift in my awareness. There was something called historical context, even when talking about God. And there was subjectivity, even when talking about eternal truths.

When the humanities course moved on to the New Testament, the effect was shattering. As he compulsively straightened and re-straightened his notes on the lectern, baby-faced Professor T. explained in the politest way possible that, over several decades following the execution of Jesus, each of the four gospels of the New Testament was written by a different person from his own distinct social, political and cultural context. Each targeted a different audience and emphasized and interpreted Jesus's message in his own nuanced ways. Although there is considerable overlap in the content of the four gospels, especially as they pertain to Jesus's death and resurrection, these four writers didn't collaborate. And many of their narrative details conflict. That was my first set of shocks. There were more to come.

Studying the four gospels carefully in turn, I was surprised by how few of the things I held to be sacred truths could be found there. The Holy Trinity, the Holy Ghost, the seven sacraments, the stations of the cross, the clergy, the monks and nuns, Sunday Mass with all the trimmings, the saints, the blessed medals and icons, the holy water, the rosary beads—all of these things that featured so prominently in my childhood faith had evolved decades or even centuries after Jesus's death, mainly after the Roman Empire converted to Christianity in the fourth century.

I had never read the Bible on my own before—it had always been interpreted for me during sermons at Mass. I now realized how selective the readings in the liturgy were. In Matthew 16:15, when Jesus asks one of his followers, Peter, "Who do you think I am?" Peter responds, "You are the Christ, the Son of the Living God." In turn, Jesus responds, "You are Peter, and upon this rock, I will build my church." The name *Peter* comes from the root word for "rock," which was why Peter would be the foundation of Jesus's church. I'd heard that line read in Mass every year of my life, as proof that Saint Peter was the first Roman Catholic pope, chosen by Jesus himself. What I hadn't realized was that it is the only line in the entire New Testament that refers to Peter having a special role in Jesus's ministry. The formidable global power of the Vatican was justified by a single line in one specific gospel, and reinforced and amplified by evolving church doctrine over many tumultuous centuries of history.

As for the Blessed Virgin Mary, I could find only two references to her being a virgin when she gave birth to Jesus, one in Matthew and one in Luke, both written decades after Jesus's death. And nowhere does it say she stayed a virgin all her life. When Professor T. made a casual reference to Jesus's many siblings, I was completely incredulous, but in fact, passages in both Matthew and Mark clearly refer to Jesus having brothers and sisters.

And Mary's Immaculate Conception—the first human to be born free from original sin—well, that wasn't anywhere in the Bible either. Nor was her "Assumption" into heaven—how she alone of all humans was able to enter the pearly gates before dying. It was personally distressing to realize how little Mary figured in the gospels at all, after everything she had meant to me. And speaking of heaven, there was scant mention of that place either. Isn't getting into heaven what life is all about? In fact, I could find almost no mention of humans even having souls. There was nothing like the constant reference to souls you find in all those so-called pagan cultures—the Greeks, Egyptians and Hindus. Instead, the Bible refers to something called the "Resurrection of the Body," which will occur at the end of time, around the apocalypse or the second coming of Christ. But that is a completely different concept from heaven. Where was all the talk about good people who, after they die, go up to heaven to live with God and the angels and saints forever?

Even celibacy among the clergy and the infallibility of

the pope were later additions, after a thousand or more years of Roman Catholic rule. I gradually realized that there was a strong case to be made, based on the New Testament writings, that Jesus wasn't keen on orthodox religion, period. *The Sabbath was made for man*, after all, and not the other way around.

I received glowing comments and grades on my course work, and I shared them with my mother. After such a long time out of her favour, I felt that she was proud of me again, which was tremendously satisfying. But I didn't share any of this new knowledge with her, or anyone else. I didn't dwell on the personal implications of my studies at all, until they forced themselves on me suddenly, over the Christmas break of my first year. It was a brutal and blind-siding blow.

My mother had always tried with all her heart to bring the traditions of Christmas into our home. She would begin secretive shopping for her seven children months in advance. We always had a beautiful real Christmas tree, decorated with shimmering tinsel and strings of beads, and red and gold balls and bells and wooden trinkets. She would wrap wreaths and garland around every banister and archway. After midnight on Christmas Eve, she would bring out our brightly wrapped presents from her hiding spot in the crawlspace and carefully stack them under the tree. Throughout Christmas Day, there would be carols playing on the hi-fi and classic Christmas movies on TV. We would eat sugar cookies with icing and sprinkles, and chocolate squares with cherries and cheesecake. We always had my mother's much-loved Acadian meat pies at Christmas lunch.

But on this Christmas Eve, during Midnight Mass, surrounded on both sides in the pew by my siblings, I listened to the reading of the nativity story from the Gospel According to Luke, and rather than experiencing the traditional joy and magic, I felt sick. I became so deeply depressed I could barely stay standing during the Our Father. When we finally got home, I rushed into the house and up to my bedroom and closed the door behind me. I cried silently, crushed and utterly alone in my grief.

The ramifications of Professor T.'s lectures had finally sunk in. How could Jesus's birth story, the foundation of Christmas, possibly be true? Why did the authors of the gospels of Matthew and Luke give such different accounts, one with shepherds watching over their sheep at night when angels appeared to them, and the other with three wise men following a star? And both gospels flashed forward from Jesus's birth to his adulthood. It made no sense that Jesus's birth would be marked with celestial signs and miracles only to have him slip into obscurity for the next 30 years before re-emerging as the Messiah and son of God. And why did the other authors of the New Testament not mention Jesus's birth at all? Was the whole birth story just a myth? Wishful thinking? Why had I taken everything so literally?

In the middle of that night, I sat alone in the family room on the couch across from the Christmas tree lights shining in a dark corner and ached with a devastating loss. I desperately wanted to hold on to the magic of the baby born in the manger. I wanted to keep believing, but now I couldn't. I was still only barely aware of the impact this would have on my most private and devastating doubt: if Jesus's birth story wasn't true, perhaps mine wasn't either.

In the new year, I read through Matthew's latest fountain-penned missive. His last words struck a more personal note than ever before.

"Let me say that I'm doing this as a last attempt because I know that you are getting tired of me and I apologize. In fact, I probably don't have the right to take the role of a big brother."

Perhaps he had seen this coming, but I was much too proud to share the crisis in my Catholic faith with him, to admit the damage that had already been done, the sense of loss I was now enduring.

"Gail, of all the friends back home, the one I'm most concerned about is you."

15

REQUIEM

MY CONFIDENCE IN THE CATHOLIC CHURCH HAD
been badly shaken, but I kept it to myself. I wasn't about to
stop attending Mass on Sundays with my family. The fear of
missing weekly Mass still went very deep, deeper than my
love of any particular tenet of Catholic faith. I could not
imagine my life without some kind of religious practice, any
more than I could imagine myself without my miracle birth.
Most of all, though, I was simply too afraid of God's disapproval, and perhaps more so, my mother's disapproval, to
abandon the church. I kept quiet, and continued to practise
my Catholicism so that no one would guess the reformation
growing inside me.

One outcome of my teenage battles with my mother over
dating Angelo was that my relationship with my older sisters
improved. All that conflict had seriously tarnished my halo

and damaged my status as the special child. Linda was now married to her high school sweetheart, Steve, and Glenna had moved to another city to attend university and was enjoying a lively social life. To them, I must have finally seemed pretty human after all, and they liked me better that way.

I secretly continued to write to the other Gail in my journal, just to review my day or the latest thing weighing on my mind, but rarely did her death or my birth come up in family conversation. Meanwhile, Jeannie, with whom I'd always shared similar interests, had grown into a reserved teen with consistently high grades who didn't date during high school. In contrast to mine, her teenage relationship with our mother was trouble-free. She had also become best friends with Angelo's two sisters. Melanie and John got on well with Angelo too, all three working part-time at my father's gas station. My personal life had finally settled down, though I still spent all of my spare time at home in my bed-room behind a closed door.

Linda and Steve were living in Barrie, a town an hour north of Toronto. She wanted more than anyone I've ever known to be a mother. After two years of trying to get pregnant, she was put on fertility pills, and finally conceived. She beamed through her pregnancy. We were all so excited for them. This would be the first grandchild, and the first nephew or niece in our family.

Linda finally hit her due date. Then another week crawled by. The days seemed to pass desperately slowly. Toward the end of that second week, during a scheduled medical appointment, the doctor couldn't find a heartbeat. Her baby had died.

Linda was in severe shock. Her doctor elected to induce labour, and began to prep her for the natural childbirth of her dead child.

I took the day off school so that I could join my mother on the trip north to the Barrie hospital. We rode in silence, both struck dumb. We arrived to find Linda sitting up in the hospital bed, touching up her makeup. Her eyes looked huge and wild and glassy, and when she saw my mother, she tried to smile. I knew immediately that the lipstick and blush were for my mother's benefit, an effort to appear strong and in control in the middle of this maelstrom. I wondered whether she truly understood what was happening.

I was surprised by my mother's strange stoicism. Her eldest daughter's baby, her first grandchild, had died, but throughout that horrible, unreal day, her pale face remained frozen, her teeth clenched tight, and her whole body was stiff. She clutched her purse in arms held tight to her stomach. I don't remember her even embracing Linda.

My mother and I weren't allowed in the maternity ward once the labour had begun. We walked around town, ate lunch in the depressingly grey hospital cafeteria, sat in the small waiting room reading old magazines. Our breathing was shallow, inhaling by the teaspoonful.

Many hours later, Steve came to find us. The baby had been born. He broke down in loud sobs.

"She was beautiful," he kept repeating, his shoulders shaking, his head bowed, his hands covering his face. "She looked just like Linda. She was beautiful."

A dark-haired baby girl. It was only then, when Steve broke down, that my mother put her arms around him, fighting back tears too.

They named the baby girl Emily. There was a private funeral service that only Linda and Steve attended. They were obliged to bury the stillborn baby in an unmarked grave.

Though she kept up a brave face for others, in the weeks and months following Emily's death, Linda felt she might lose her mind. Many years later, she told me she was plagued by nightmares, and after several months of intense grief, she broke down in front of our mother and confessed that she wasn't coping. But instead of sympathy, Linda sensed a sort of impatience, as though our mother had hoped Linda would have begun to move on from the tragedy by then. She offered few words of consolation. Instead, she recommended that Linda have a heart-to-heart talk with me. She said I was studying a lot of religious texts at university, and that I might be able to offer some words of wisdom that would give her spiritual support.

Linda was crushed. She'd reached out to her mother and been redirected to her favoured little sister. She didn't follow up on our mother's advice, didn't seek me out, and continued to suffer in silence and isolation.

꙰

When I thought back to my earliest memories of my mother, I had no impression of a woman who was carrying around the uniquely devastating pain that comes with the loss of a child. I was unaware of my parents ever visiting the other Gail's grave. I saw no evidence of mourning at all. Yes, my birth still struck me as a miracle, pure and simple. Only a true miracle would be capable of washing away a mother's inconsolable anguish for her dead baby only a year after the death occurred. Only the true belief in a miracle.

Years later, I came to see my mother's failure to share too closely in Linda's tragedy as a defence mechanism. I think she was afraid of reawakening her own pain, that delirious grief that she'd been able to bury so deep.

Had I known about my mother's recommendation to Linda at the time, I might have realized that, at the age of nineteen, I was undergoing a restoration in my mother's eyes. Despite my private crisis of faith, I was re-emerging as the family's official anointed one.

16

CHRISTOLOGY

IT WAS A BEAUTIFUL, BRILLIANTLY SUNNY DAY IN the late spring of my first year at York. I was shuffling out of a crowded lecture hall, deep in thought, when Professor T. called after me and gestured for me to wait while he packed up his lecture notes and answered questions from lingering students. I was startled. I'd never spoken to him before, and there was no reason he should even know my name. I stood near the door and waited, mouth dry and heart racing.

He asked if he could join me as we were both headed in the same direction across campus. As we set out, he told me that all year long he'd noticed me sitting alone high up in the lecture hall, and was always struck by how intensely I was listening. He said that sometimes my concentration was so focused, the eye contact so steady, that it was almost as though, in that crowded hall, he was speaking directly to me. I was surprised and embarrassed.

"The truth is I'm supposed to wear eyeglasses for distances, but I don't usually bother in lectures, so most of the time, I can barely see your face, let alone your eyes," I said, laughing nervously.

There was a moment of awkward silence during which I hated myself. I had tried to be self-deprecating, but instead my response had been ungracious.

Then he continued, saying he'd done a bit of a background check on me. My tutorial leader had praised me. My essays and class participation were excellent. I was an A student. He asked what subject I was planning to major in, and I told him political science.

"Well, I wanted to let you know that I'm offering a second-year humanities course next year that will delve a lot deeper into the subject of the historical Jesus, and how Jesus has been interpreted throughout Western literature. You might consider signing up, because you seem to have a strong affinity for this material."

He invited me to come by his office to discuss it further. Then, smiling and squinting in the bright sunlight, he told me he liked the way the sun brought out the red highlights in my hair. I thanked him, but I had recently put a henna rinse in my hair, and all I could think was that my red highlights were fake.

The following week, I dropped by Professor T.'s office. He

spoke with enthusiasm about his course on the historical Jesus and pulled a few books from the reading list off his bookshelf and offered them to me. One was a personal copy of J.D. Salinger's *Franny and Zooey* with a few yellow marker highlights and margin notes. He mentioned that he was teaching another course in the coming year that I should also consider signing up for, a humanities class on the concept of love through the ages, in philosophy, theology, psychology and literature. Soon after, I signed up for both.

When I came home from the meeting with that armful of books, my mother seemed impressed that a university professor had taken such a personal interest in me. But when Glenna came home for a visit from her out-of-town university the following weekend, she offered a different view.

"Professors don't give students they hardly know free books for no good reason," she said, laughing and rolling her eyes.

The inference was obvious. She wondered how I could possibly be so naive. I wondered why she had to be so cynical. She knew absolutely nothing about him. I was mainly infuriated that she would question Professor T.'s noble intentions in front of my mother, whom I was eager to impress.

That summer, I read *Franny and Zooey*, and it opened up a whole new way for me to re-embrace Christianity. At its best, Christianity was focused on *this* world, not on the next. It was about human relationships, not doctrine. The sacred was within the secular. The Kingdom of God was in the midst of us. This was just the kind of Christianity I needed.

Early in my second year at York, I formally switched my major from political science to religious studies, and Professor T. became my academic advisor. Although his textual analysis of the New Testament further eroded my confidence in the authority of the Catholic Church, it raised my esteem for the historical, flesh-and-blood Jesus. Jesus was so radical, so unique, so enlightened that it was no wonder the early Christians constantly misunderstood and misrepresented him. I was rediscovering Jesus as the most profound and provocative poet the world has ever known.

I was so inspired by Professor T. that I was able to distract myself from the traumatic loss of my traditional faith. This new Christian world view had no particular need for the "miracles, mystery and authority" of the church, to quote the Dostoyevsky novel on Professor T.'s reading list. I didn't want to dwell on whether I still believed I was the miraculous rebirth of the other Gail. What was most critical, now, was that my mother still believed it.

I was getting consistent As on essays and tests. In the margin of a paper I wrote on the metaphor of sight in the New Testament, Professor T. wrote:

> *This is a brilliant insight into the meaning of "see" in this*
> *saying. Your essay makes it possible to get a fresh understanding*
> *of Jesus' message. You've helped me to "see" more clearly some*
> *things I was seeing only dimly. This is an outstanding piece &*
> *is a good example of your extraordinary gifts of understanding.*

I felt overwhelmed and exhilarated by his approval, as though this was what I'd always longed for. I showed his comments to my mother. She seemed equally awed. I was gaining a reputation in my family for my academic performance, something I hadn't particularly enjoyed since I was a child. Jeannie had always been the stronger student, but she was a few years behind me, still in high school, and overshadowed by my recent performance.

A new sense of purpose was taking hold of me. Perhaps I was meant to be not a martyr or a saint but a philosopher. In my most unguarded moments, I imagined being one of the great scholars of the late-twentieth century. Like Kant or Marx, I wanted to impact the course of modern Western thought.

⤙

Not all of my ambition was so lofty. I had recently turned twenty, and most people my age already had their driving licences. I was determined to get mine too, and had booked my first in-car lesson. Sitting in the driver's seat, the instructor in the passenger seat next to me, I managed to back out of my house's driveway. I slowly drove a block, but that was as far as I got before I froze in a panic attack and the car began to drift toward the curb. The instructor insisted I brake, turn off the engine and get out. He wanted us to switch seats. I wasn't ready to learn to drive at this time, he said, and he wasn't willing to take me out again. He urged me to consider class instruction before ever trying to get behind a wheel again.

I began to wonder if I was unconsciously remembering the car accident from my previous life as the other Gail. It led me to view my rebirth differently, in a way that still affirmed my mother's story. This was the 1970s, and reincarnation was a cool Eastern doctrine that was beginning to gain traction in Western pop culture. I began to think of myself as the reincarnation of the other Gail, which felt somehow less melodramatic to me than being a miracle child that God brought back from the dead just for my mother. Reincarnation wasn't a Catholic doctrine, which meant it wasn't dependent on my teetering faith in the church. It wasn't even Christian. In fact, reincarnation didn't require any divine intervention at all. It didn't require prayer or gratitude. It carried no obligations, no strings, no expectations or disappointments. Reincarnation could just happen, to anyone. I secretly began to use the language of reincarnation in my head when I thought of myself and my dead sister. It was a subtle but substantial shift. Sometimes, even talking to a near stranger, I began to practise my new theory. "I am the reincarnation of my sister, who was a car accident victim, and this has affected my ability to learn to drive."

For the very first time in my life, I had found an impersonal language to contain my most intimate truth. I still addressed my journals to the other Gail, but I was less inclined to think of her as a soul in heaven. I had reverted back to thinking of us as a single person, one continuous soul with two births. I was hoping this might relieve some of my performance pressure, but it didn't work.

I didn't really need my driver's licence anyway. Angelo drove me everywhere. Part chauffeur, part bodyguard, he made a long detour every weekday morning to get me from my house to the York campus, and he drove me home at the end of each day. And I never needed to go anywhere after school—I spent most of my time in my bedroom doing school work, only sewing to take a break. My grades were all that mattered now.

17

REVELATION

MY PRIDE IN MY ACADEMIC PERFORMANCE QUICKLY converted itself into a more heightened state of anxiety. Anything less than an A was a failure. I worried about every assignment, every test and every tutorial. I was starting to suspect there was something wrong with me, a streak of masochism at the base of my fears. The better my academic performance, the more I was at risk of being a hopeless disappointment. I was becoming a nervous wreck.

Angelo began to express concern about my stress level. I was always agitated and obsessing over my school work, no matter how well I did. He urged me to make an appointment with his family doctor, who was studying psychology and had begun to see patients for counselling. I was reluctant, but Angelo nagged me until I finally agreed.

I met with the aspiring psychologist only once. He said I

was living my life as if I were walking on a balance beam, thinking the beam was hundreds of feet in the air when, all the while, it was only a few inches from the ground. My anxiety came from the mistaken belief that a single slip would have fatal consequences, that there was something "life or death" about staying on that beam. He seemed sincere and eager to help, but I left his office with no intention of returning. What did he know about how far I could fall? What did he know about how much was at stake?

I drank too much coffee, had trouble sleeping and lost weight. I worried constantly about whether I was good enough to study with Professor T. I feared being a disappointment to him. I felt indebted to him for his attention and approval. I felt unworthy.

Dear Gail, I always feel like he's seeing through me, finding faults and flaws—I feel like he sees the real me—weak and full of pride.

I became obsessed with the idea that familiarity breeds contempt. The more Professor T. got to know me, the more he would see that I was not the person he thought I was, that he had been mistaking me for someone else. People were always mistaking me for someone else. I could make a good first impression, but I'd wind up being nothing but a letdown.

There were a number of undergraduate students at York who hovered around Professor T. like disciples—male and female, older and younger. They were bright, witty, sophisticated, cool and confident. Like me, they found his classes intellectually stimulating and provocative, but unlike me, they smiled with him as though they shared a joke the rest of the world didn't quite get. There was an atmosphere of fellowship, and sometimes a near-giddy excitement surrounding him.

I couldn't quite relate to these students, even though I admired them tremendously. They were friendly and sometimes invited me to socialize with them, but I always declined. Outside of the classroom, I continued to keep to myself. The less others knew about the real me, the better. A few of the older students enjoyed Professor T.'s lectures so much they audited classes they'd already taken. One mysterious woman who was five or ten years older than the rest of us attended every one of his lectures without even being registered as a student. She stood out due to the style of her clothes—she was a preppie, girlish California hippy. She always wore striking pink or powder-blue mini skirts and tights, and pink silk scarves like a cap on top of her long, pale-blonde hair. I heard other students refer to her simply as "the pink lady."

Professor T. invited me to apply for an advanced seminar course he was offering the following year that would get to the very heart of his personal research and expertise. It would expose his most gifted inner circle of students to graduate-level work. Enrolment was by personal invitation only.

Near the end of my second year, when regular classes had finished, I needed to get my third-year course selection signed by Professor T., as my academic advisor. He suggested that I bring the sheet to his house in downtown Toronto, rather than both of us travelling all the way up to the York campus just for a signature. He said he sometimes saw other students at his home instead of at his office.

Angelo was wary of Professor T., of course. He distrusted the intentions of men in general, and I was used to this. He asked how long the meeting would take and I guessed about twenty minutes. He said he'd meet me at a nearby subway station when it was over.

I arrived to find Professor T. in good spirits, almost bouncing, eyes shining. He brought me into the living room and invited me to sit down on his "love seat." It was the first time I'd heard that phrase. The lights in the room were low but the sun's rays cut through the front window and across the room. He had crystal liquor glasses set out and quickly poured two drinks. I think it was sherry. He sat opposite me in a high-backed armchair. I asked after his wife and son. He said they were away. He moved to a different seat, saying he liked how the light from the front window fell on me and he wanted a better angle to appreciate it. I became self-conscious. I took the sheet out of my bag and began nervously reviewing my courses with him. He listened politely. Then he suggested I join him in the kitchen, because he was going to do a little advance preparation for our dinner. I was confused. I followed him into the kitchen and, to my horror, there were two thick raw steaks resting on the counter. I couldn't have been more surprised. I immediately thought of Angelo, probably already waiting for me at the subway station. Professor T. was talking enthusiastically about how he was going to prepare the steaks when I managed to stutter an interruption.

"I'm sorry, but I didn't realize you thought I was coming over for dinner. I can't stay. I have to be somewhere else soon."

Now it was his turn to be surprised. He looked flustered, and muttered that he'd felt sure he had mentioned to me that it was a dinner invitation. He often made dinner for visiting students, he said.

"No problem." He grabbed the steaks from the counter and practically threw them into the fridge.

We went back to the living room. The atmosphere had changed completely, and was now awkward and tense. I apologized again, feeling awful, hoping the steaks wouldn't go to waste. I was sure the misunderstanding had been my fault. I must have misheard when we spoke over the phone about the course sheet.

"No big deal," he said, almost dismissively, although his face had gone dark. Then he began to ask me questions. Had I heard something about him? Some gossip?

"No," I assured him, "I've heard nothing."

That was true. I wasn't privy to any kind of gossip. I couldn't even imagine what he was talking about. He then asked me whether people were gossiping about "the pink lady," though he called her by her proper name. I told him no, though that wasn't quite true. I had noticed a little snickering among one or two other students, but only about her style of dress.

I checked my watch and apologized that I had to go, and apologized again for the misunderstanding about dinner. As I squeezed past him in his narrow entrance hall and made my way out his front door, I felt anger radiating from him, though I wasn't sure if it was directed at me specifically. I rushed down his street toward the subway, grateful to Angelo for having provided me with the excuse to leave. The whole experience had felt uncomfortable.

A few months later, at the start of the new school year, I was apprehensive about seeing Professor T. again. Nothing inappropriate had happened between us, but I still felt a lingering embarrassment at the memory. As it turned out, our interactions were largely unchanged. I maintained an appropriate professional distance and he did the same. I resolved to avoid any potential misunderstandings in the future.

Professor T.'s new seminar was exhilarating, and my enthusiasm for an academic career in religious studies was growing. The class was sharp, entertaining and had great energy. I felt honoured to be engaged in something so important, so authentic, but despite this, I remained anxious and strung out, and drank coffee instead of eating.

⤙

It happened suddenly, with a phone call late one afternoon near the end of my third year. I took the call standing at the kitchen doorway, my mother nearby. She must have sensed something, because she hovered. The voice belonged to one of the students in Professor T.'s inner circle, not someone I knew well, who quickly apologized for having to ask me a very personal question.

"Have you experienced any sexual advances or been sexually involved with Professor T. while you've been enrolled in his classes?"

I heard the words but I simply couldn't find my voice. The caller quickly added that a number of female students were speaking up about having had sexual experiences with Professor T. Might I be one of them? There was a long pause. I still said nothing, as if any response from me would make this phone call real.

"Because, down the road, it might become necessary to approach the university with a formal complaint against him. With signatures."

I fought to stay upright, feet planted on the kitchen floor, phone held tightly in my hand, simply horrified. I finally forced out a response.

"No."

I could think of nothing else to say. I sensed some relief on the other end of the line.

"Okay. Thank you. Maybe without even realizing it, you managed to keep him in his proper place. You probably did him a big favour."

We hung up. Before I could catch myself, I started to choke and sob violently, blurting out to my mother that

Professor T. had been sleeping with his female students. In my peripheral vision, I saw her jerk toward me, but I turned away and ran up to my bedroom. I stopped at the top of the staircase and turned back to see her stricken face at the kitchen door.

"Please don't tell Glenna," I begged her.

Once I had closed myself up in my bedroom, the caller's words began to sink in. I had completely idealized him. I had honestly believed that he was pure and good, and inspired by a higher truth. Like a prophet for a new age, he had offered me hope when my old foundations were crumbling. Now, I felt appalled and betrayed that his sights weren't set so high after all. I was deeply disappointed in him and morally offended by his apparent promiscuity, but what angered me most was my own naïveté, my eagerness to believe in him, my anxious desire for his approval. How could I have been so utterly blind? I was ashamed at my poor judgment, and I felt stupid. Profoundly stupid.

An hour passed before I could calm myself down and leave my bedroom. When I did, I held my head high.

"It's okay," I told my mother. "Life will go on."

She looked so distraught. I didn't want her to worry about me, but neither did I want to talk about it. I didn't want to even think about it. I was determined to put the whole shocking revelation out of my head.

I only ever spoke with one fellow student about the infamous phone call. She admitted to having had an affair with

Professor T. several years before, and spoke of how emotionally damaging it had been at the time. But she said she'd continued to take his courses after their sexual relationship was over because he was such a great teacher.

My third-year classes were over now and I wouldn't have to face Professor T. anytime soon. I threw all of my energy into studying for my remaining exams. I had an enormous amount of work to keep me occupied. After one exam, an English professor asked to have a word with me in his office. I sat in a chair across from his desk. He wanted to know if I'd ever considered doing graduate work in English literature. He thought I would be an excellent candidate. I immediately broke down crying. He was startled and fumbled awkwardly through an apology, terribly sorry if he'd said anything that had put unnecessary pressure on me. I shook my head. I told him it was just that I wasn't getting much sleep, that was all. I left his office quickly, overwhelmed by the sudden realization that I no longer knew what to do with my life.

⤙

Matthew and I had rarely corresponded since my first year at York. Now, after a long silence, I received a letter from him in the mail. He sounded distressed, unhappy with his schooling and was wrestling with thoughts about his future.

"I seem to be going from one crisis to another," he wrote,

"wondering which is the best life—contemplative, intellectual, apostolic, etc."

He was at a crossroads. Perhaps he was unsure whether God was calling him to a life in the church after all.

There was something different about him. His message was more personal.

"I realize now that you are a rare find," he went on, "and I think it a shame that we both live so close to one another and not at least write. Perhaps, though, the quote may apply: 'you can never go back again.' I don't know about that but I do know that I still value your friendship above all the other ones I have—and I'm pretty sure that is the truth."

The letter was signed, "Love Matthew." He'd never signed that way before. I took the regret I felt rising up when I thought about him and pushed it back, deep down. I was in the middle of a crisis of my own, one I could never, would never, share with him. I was too ashamed. Besides, I couldn't believe Matthew saw the real me when he thought of me, only the person he wanted to see. The real me was someone he could never love.

18

MORTIFICATION

A HOUSE SOUNDS SO DIFFERENT IN THE DEAD OF night—the clock on the kitchen wall, the refrigerator motor, the creaks and heaves. An hour would go by. I'd pull my rosary out from under my pillow and recite Hail Marys. True, I now knew that the Blessed Virgin Mary was an entirely non-Biblical construct, heavily drawn from pagan female deities like the Egyptian goddess Isis, and slowly developed by the church over centuries after the conversion of Rome. There was barely anything about Mary in the gospels or epistles to hang a hope on. And yet, the thought of Mary could still offer me solace, and reciting the Hail Mary was much more comforting than counting sheep.

But still not good enough. After a few more hours had passed, I would usually get up, place my pillow at the foot of my bed and switch places, my blankets pulled over me. I would imagine I was floating in the bottom of a small boat on a river, like the Lady of Shalott. After another hour or two, I'd get up and place my pillow back at the top of the bed again. Now I lay on my back, hands folded on my chest like a dead person in an open casket. Sometimes I'd tiptoe downstairs in the middle of the night and make camomile tea or warm up a cup of milk in a small saucer on the stove. Once or twice I slipped down into the dark basement in my pyjamas, barefoot on the cold ceramic tile floor, looking for dregs of alcohol in the old bottles behind the bar. These were ancient bottles, long drained in small secret shots by my father, with only foul-tasting sediment in their glass bottoms.

Sometimes, I was still awake at 6 a.m. when the alarm clock in my parents' room sounded faintly. The last thing I would remember before finally falling into a deep sleep was hearing my dad head to the bathroom to shower, only to have my own alarm clock wake me an hour later. I wasn't aware of anything in particular on my mind. This was just how my nights were now.

My mother knew that I was having difficulty sleeping, though we didn't talk about why. After three weeks of severe insomnia, she suggested I make an appointment with the family doctor. He was a gruff, crusty old guy. I asked him if I could have a prescription for sleeping pills. He looked squarely at me and asked, "What's happened?" I was planning to say something vague, but my distress over the news about Professor T., suppressed for weeks, suddenly emerged and betrayed me. For the first time since the phone call, I burst into tears. I heard myself admitting that a professor I had hugely admired was accused of being sexually involved with a bunch of students. It was only in that moment that I had made the connection between Professor T. and my insomnia. My doctor asked if I'd been sexually involved with this professor myself and I quickly shook my head. Then I felt even more embarrassed for crying. He gave me a prescription for sedatives to be taken before bed, and I went home feeling shaken awake by my own confession.

The news about Professor T. had clearly affected me more deeply than I'd realized. But it wasn't only my profound disappointment in him. I was disappointed in myself. I had been seduced by his attention, by his charisma, by his provocative and liberating interpretation of the Bible. I had believed what I wanted to believe about him, because he'd made me feel special. I blamed myself.

⤙

I began a summer job as a file clerk at a company called United Tire and Rubber that manufactured off-the-road tires for construction and agricultural companies. I filed their paper invoices in colour-coded folders, eight hours a day, five days a week. It was the perfect job for my current level of emotional energy.

A young man named Gordon, a few years older than me,

worked in the credit department, calling customers who were behind on their payments. His voice carried through the open office. He was eccentric in word and manner, blunt and witty, his rapid-fire sentences filled with puns and wise-cracks. Perhaps it was because he'd been raised in England, living above a pub managed by his father, but he could be off-colour, irreverent and ribald. He was always making play-ful sound effects, indulging in word play, quoting Monty Python with accompanying accents. His smart-ass quips and candour offended some co-workers and amused others. "Fuck 'em if they can't take a joke," he'd say.

He heard I was studying religion in university and was intrigued. He'd been raised with very little religious instruc-tion or practice. With a devilish grin on his face, he'd ask if Catholics slaughtered chickens on the altar during Mass. He wanted to know what I thought about aliens from outer space having built the pyramids of Egypt. He walked up to my desk one day, leaned in closely as if to get personal, and asked me if I thought beauty was a gift from God. I was embarrassed, not sure if he was implying something about me or not.

But Gordon also asked me real questions about my stud-ies, and I surprised myself by opening up about Professor T. when I'd barely discussed the scandal with Angelo. I'd been afraid that Angelo would misinterpret the nature of my dis-tress. But Gordon was a near stranger when I told him how, after studying with Professor T. for three years, I was devastated to learn of his apparent sexual involvement with some of his students.

"Well, did anything good come from taking his courses?" Gordon asked.

"Yes," I admitted. "I learned an enormous amount."

"Then stop dwelling on the negative." He practically barked it at me as he turned on his heel and returned to his desk.

I didn't know what to think of Gordon. He could be quite irritating, and a breath of very fresh air at the same time. He seemed truly disinterested in what other people thought of him, almost oblivious, but his attitude toward the world seemed liberating. I realized I could use a little of that attitude myself.

19

REDEMPTION

I WAS ABOUT TO TURN TWENTY-TWO THAT SUMMER, and Angelo asked how I'd feel about getting a diamond engagement ring for my birthday. My school work had pushed marriage to the back of my mind in the last few years, but my recent emotional chaos now made the idea appealing. Marriage was just the thing to bring some stability to my life. One by one, my old grade school friends were getting engaged and married, and it seemed like a natural move forward for us too. We picked the ring out together and settled on a simple solitaire. I thought it was beautiful and I loved looking at it on my finger. I wasn't ready to set a date, but this meant we were one step closer to the sacrament of matrimony.

I was thinking about my future in a whole new way. Long gone was my fantasy about becoming a nun. In fact, God no longer figured into my future plans at all. Now I wanted to be an academic, and I was imagining marriage, a home of my own, children. And normalcy had never looked so attractive.

Days after my birthday, I got a surprise phone call from Matthew. It had been a few years since I'd heard his voice. He was talking fast about being back in the city, wondering if I'd go with him to see a Shakespeare play at the Stratford Festival, a couple of hours' drive out of town. We could make a whole day of it.

I was stunned. I immediately thought of Angelo, and how upset he'd be if I went on a day's outing with Matthew. How could I possibly say yes? But then I saw myself sitting in the passenger seat of Matthew's car on the highway, just the two of us, or in a café, or on a park bench by the river that ran through the town of Stratford. It had been ages since I'd seen him. I had a powerful flashback to those wonderful hours we'd spent in the high school library.

But there wasn't really any choice in my mind. I had to tell Matthew I couldn't go.

"Last week, Angelo and I got officially engaged," I said. "So I don't think it would be a good idea. I'm sorry, Matthew." There was a horrible moment of dead air, followed by a polite exchange of goodbyes.

It wasn't until I hung up that the surprise began to sink in. Had Matthew just asked me out on a *date*? After all these years? I had given up on him long ago, and had emotionally prepared myself for his ordination into the priesthood. Was he looking to test his faith? Was I to be that last temptation before he took his vows? Or was the invitation nothing more than an innocent impulse inspired by a beautiful summer day?

What weighed heaviest was the thought that he might seriously be thinking about rejecting the priesthood in favour of a more ordinary life. If so, was he thinking, after all these years, of a life with me? Beginning with Shakespeare? I couldn't think straight. Weren't we soul mates in a way that Angelo and I had never been? Didn't I owe him a day to talk about it at least, even as a friend? I feared that I'd just made a tragic mistake. I should have said yes. No matter what it meant. No matter what happened. *Is it too late to change my mind? Should I call him back?* But how could I say yes now that he knew about my engagement? He would only be disappointed by my lack of loyalty.

He wrote a letter to me soon afterwards.

"I want to congratulate you and Angelo and I wish you two the greatest happiness possible. As for myself, I admit that I was and am attracted to you, but believe me, your engagement, although a surprise to me, does not affect how I feel or shall act towards you because I have always cherished our friendship and want to do nothing to jeopardize it."

He had used the word *attracted* for the very first time.

He continued:

"It has always been my experience that whenever I have talked with you, the joy and happiness I have felt as a result prompt me to think: if life can be so rewarding and fulfilling in just the simple enjoyment of being with someone one loves, imagine the magnitude of the joy one should (and would I feel) receive if he were to try to establish a relationship of love with the Father?"

A part of me hated myself for turning down Matthew's invitation, for my lack of courage, lack of openness in that critical moment. What would have been on that road I'd left untravelled? I feared I would regret not knowing for the rest of my life. I knew I couldn't even offer him friendship, not while married to Angelo. But I also feared that I might have played a part in his decision to devote his life exclusively to God after all, and that left me with an even heavier heart.

In the second-to-last day of my summer office job before returning to university for my final year, Gordon from the credit department asked if he could have a private word with me during lunch. I had no idea what this was about. We sat alone on a picnic table at the back of the office building, only a dozen yards from noisy highway traffic. He seemed agitated and cleared his throat almost theatrically, then got right to the point.

"If I were to draw up a list of all the qualities I'm looking for in a woman, you would get about 92 percent. So if you'd care to break off your engagement with Angelo to go out with me, I'd be pleased about that."

I was taken completely off guard. I tried not to laugh out loud at his business-like, matter-of-fact tone.

"Where did I lose marks?" I asked.

He thought a bit before he answered.

"Your voice," he said finally. "I find your voice a little irritating."

I thanked him politely but declined his offer. I told him I still intended to marry Angelo.

↓

I returned to university in September looking forward to a mix of courses in modern theology, modern philosophy and modern literature. No more ancients. Thanks to Professor T., I'd had enough of the so-called historical Jesus too. From now on, it would be nothing but post-Enlightenment thinkers for me. I was informed by my college master at York that he would be acting as my academic advisor during my final year because Professor T. was taking some time off.

I continued to obsess about my course work, my grades and my future. But surprisingly, I felt fine. Stranger still, I felt I owed a lot of my positive new attitude to Gordon from United Tire and Rubber. His eccentric good humour that summer had really cheered me up.

After I'd been engaged to Angelo for about six months, the issue of setting a date came up. I began stalling. I bought bridal magazines in an effort to get more into the mood, but I left them unread on my closet floor. I began to question whether I was ready to marry Angelo after all. I still had a genuine affection for him. I was still attracted to him. But we were so different. Our interests barely overlapped. There was such a large part of my inner life, my thoughts and feelings, that I didn't feel I could share with him, that I didn't think he'd ever understand. It left me feeling very alone. In the wake of emotional turmoil I'd experienced, I'd welcomed getting engaged, but marriage was forever. I began to suspect that the main thing keeping us together was my fear of how difficult it would be to break up. I couldn't face hurting him again. He deserved better.

That spring, early on a Friday evening, Angelo arrived at my house the way he'd done hundreds of times before. He was in cheerful spirits, looking forward to the start of another weekend. I met him at the side door and asked if he could come up to my bedroom. He never came into my bedroom, and besides, the floor was always cluttered with half-finished sewing projects. He was curious. He followed me upstairs, leaping two steps at a time. I shut the door behind him. I was shaking and could barely look up. I pulled the engagement ring off of my finger.

"I don't think I can marry you after all," I said.

He smiled gently, surprised but completely calm. I reached out and handed him the ring. He took it and held it in his hand. There was a moment of silence as he searched my face, then he spoke, very softly.

"I'll hold on to it for now, but I know you're just having a case of cold feet. I know this will pass. I'm not worried." There was a long pause. "Do you want me to leave now?" he asked. It was his only question that night. I nodded, grateful for his kindness.

He left the house quietly, still smiling, though I may have seen a slight quiver in his lips. His last words to me that day were that he loved me, and he reassured me that everything would be okay. I suspected he thought I was having a nervous breakdown, and that my feelings weren't really about our relationship at all.

The following day, I too feared I was breaking down. I was single for the first time in six and a half years and I was beginning to panic. But what really frightened me was backsliding on the breakup, retreating back into the safety of the past and starting the cycle of doubt again. I needed a forward focus. I impulsively pulled the huge telephone book out of the kitchen closet to look up a name and number. My call came as a shock to Gordon. It sounded like he was having an asthma attack on the other end of the line (he was, in fact, asthmatic). I asked him if he'd care to get together for a coffee next week. He said, "Sure," trying to catch his breath.

Angelo and I barely ever spoke again. I knew from family members that he was distraught. He visited one day several weeks later to plead with me to give him one more chance. He looked devastated, but he kept a modest distance between us and displayed none of the teenage anger or histrionics I'd experienced in high school four years earlier. He was respectful, and he didn't stay long.

My family was also in shock. Angelo had been a fixture in our home for more than six years, and none of them had seen this coming. He had worked part-time at my father's service station, pumping gas alongside John and Melanie. His sisters had become Jeannie's best friends, and they'd long seen themselves as sisters-in-law. Jeannie was at York University now herself, studying many of the same kinds of philosophical and literary works I'd read. Even though we didn't spend a lot of time together, we had much in common, so her disapproval was particularly distressing. My parents, too, were withdrawn and unhappy with me. My mother was icy. My father scowled. Neither asked me why, but it was just as well. Everyone had assumed I was contented in the relationship, and I didn't know how to explain the breakup without it sounding like I'd misled everyone, for years.

⤙

Within weeks, I graduated from York University with an honours BA. My mother forced my father to take time off work to attend the graduation ceremony with her. I could tell he didn't want to be there, at least partly because I'd broken up with Angelo. In addition to graduating *summa cum laude*, I won a couple of other awards, including the Dean's Award for Highest Standing in the Faculty of Arts. In a photo of us on the campus grounds, my hands are clenched in fists at my stomach. My father looks tired and irritated. But my mother is almost smiling.

20

PROVIDENCE

IN THE SPRING OF 1980, I FELT I WAS FINALLY LEAVING behind the guilt and disappointment that had weighed me down for so long. My dead sister, my miraculous birth and my failed religious vocation still reverberated somewhere inside me, but for now, they were buried deep enough to ignore. I had taken a year-long break from university to work as a file clerk for United Tire and Rubber, and I was about to get married to a man who made me laugh. I had won a prestigious special MA scholarship from the Research Council of Canada and in September I would begin graduate work in the Department of Religious Studies at McMaster University. I was looking forward to the future.

I had begun dating Gordon within a week or two of ending my engagement to Angelo. In many ways, he was Angelo's opposite. Gordon wasn't remotely sentimental or romantic.

Instead, he was cheery, chatty and sometimes cheeky. He didn't take himself too seriously, and more importantly, he didn't take me too seriously either. He found humour in everything, high and low. I found his character enormously liberating, as though a great and solemn weight had been lifted from my shoulders.

Within three or four months of dating, I began to think seriously about marrying Gordon, and I let him know it. Marriage now represented freedom, freedom from my old self, a radical breakout from the prison of my past. I wanted to move out of my parents' house. I wanted independence. I wanted to be different. I wanted to be someone new.

Gordon was caught off guard by my impatience, and anxious about being rushed to the altar. He had been happily single, living at home with his widowed mother and spending most of his money and free time on cars and with friends who liked cars as much as he did. By contrast, I had been in a serious relationship since I was sixteen. I pressured Gordon and within weeks had worn him down.

I felt little sentimentality about getting married, but plenty of joy and excitement. In our marriage, there would likely be no mushy, gushing declarations or wild passions. "I love you" never passed Gordon's lips. But I knew he loved me, and I thought he would be good for me. He was consistently cheerful, good-hearted, clever and pragmatic. I needed that.

Our wedding would be a Catholic service, but I wanted there to be modifications. Instead of getting married at my family's parish, I chose the ultra-modern, non-denominational chapel at York University. I also decided that I wanted to be "given away" by both parents. My mother and father and I would walk down the aisle together, our arms linked. It made no sense to have my father give me away alone—not only because it was a sexist tradition but because my mother had always been so central in my life. I wanted her to share in that symbolic gesture.

Sitting around the crowded kitchen dinner table on a Sunday evening, only a couple of weeks before the big day, my siblings and I sparred for attention in the usual ways, competing with news and gossip and wisecracks. There were still five of us kids living at home. I chirped away about last-minute wedding details. I had finally finished sewing my wedding dress. I was feeling great.

I was blindsided when, toward the end of the meal, my father broke his usual silence by turning to me and saying, "Gail, I'm not sure this marriage of yours is going to last."

I felt my face go hot. He'd never said anything so personal to me before. And he'd said it at the dinner table, in front of everyone else. He was no longer drinking as much as he used to on Sundays, so I couldn't blame it on the beer.

"Don't get me wrong," he continued. "I like Gordon. He's a nice guy. I just think you don't have enough in common."

I was livid. Didn't he know that opposites attract? Couldn't he see how much happier I was now? Of course not. He'd never paid attention to me before, so why start now? I couldn't bring myself to respond, for fear I would lose control and become too emotional.

Instead, I said nothing, and neither did anyone else, including my mother, who just stared down at her plate. After an awkward moment, Melanie changed the subject; the conversation picked up again and ran happily off in another direction. I waited a moment, then casually got up and left the table. I didn't want anyone to know how upset I was. My dad and I rarely spoke at the best of times, but now we would be speaking even less.

Even today, I ask myself why he said it. What was the point of expressing his doubt in front of everyone like that, and so close to my wedding day? Was he the only one who thought this? Or just the only one who cared enough to be honest with me? Was it just to get his opinion on the record, so later he could say "I told you so"? Because he never did say "I told you so." That wasn't his style.

My mother offered no criticism of the eccentric new man in my life. I was grateful to her for that, knowing how caustic she'd been in the past when she didn't approve of something or someone. After all, Gordon wasn't even Catholic. But she was quite friendly toward him, and even seemed occasionally amused by him. More surprising still, she seemed to accept our impulsive engagement. We never talked about it openly, of course, but perhaps she could see that I was happier than I'd been in many years. Or perhaps she no longer had as much energy for conflict. She was mellowing, at least toward me.

⤙

Matthew and I exchanged letters one last time, just after my wedding. I wrote to tell him about my marriage, not to Angelo but to Gordon. He wrote back to congratulate me, expressing no surprise at my husband's name change. In that letter, he also told me he was going on a vocational retreat later that summer:

"If all goes well according to my hopes, I shall enter the order after the retreat. It's a monastic order, the Carthusians to be exact."

The Carthusians? That was the strictest Catholic monastic order on the planet. Carthusians take a vow of silence and solitude, living in small cells and spending all their time in reading and contemplating Holy Scripture, in communion with the Heavenly Father. They are completely cut off from the outside world in every respect. For a guy who loved to talk, often at breakneck speed, a vow of silence sounded like an unimaginable sacrifice.

He signed the letter: "I wish you every happiness and joy and may the Immaculate Heart of Mary and the Sacred Heart of Jesus be your strength and consolation. Sincerely, Matthew."

Then, it was as if he had died. I worried that he'd become a Carthusian monk after all. As years went by, I wondered what happened to him more and more. When I crossed paths with a former high school classmate, I asked if she knew anything. She said she'd heard a rumour that he was an ordained priest, and a member of Opus Dei. What a relief, I thought. Being in Opus Dei meant he was still talking, and perhaps in a position of great power in the Vatican. That thought amused me.

⤙

Moving out of my parents' house and into a small apartment with Gordon was, as I expected, the most liberating experience I'd ever known. If I needed any proof that my psychological problems were behind me, it came soon after, when I obtained my driver's licence. My anxiety about reliving the horrible car accident had evaporated. And my more introverted tendencies were changing too. Gordon and I began throwing dinner parties for old school friends, and I was happily socializing, as I hadn't done in many years. During that first year of marriage, I also completed my master's degree with first-class standing in religious studies at McMaster University, devouring my course work with enthusiasm. I really did feel brand new.

I started skipping regular church service on Sundays. Gordon, disinterested in organized religion and irreverent by nature, wasn't about to attend with me. Faced with going alone, my resolve weakened. As a child, I'd attended Mass on week-days alone, just for the pleasure of it. Now, while the inside of a Catholic church still felt like hallowed ground, the meaning of the ancient words of the liturgy and the lyrics of the hymns grated on my nerves. But staying home instead wasn't easy for me—my Sunday mornings now took on a strange spirit of disquiet.

As difficult as it was to skip Sunday Mass, missing my mother's Sunday dinner was impossible. I went home to see her weekly. I didn't tell her that I wasn't attending Mass, and she didn't ask. I suspected that she suspected.

21

DISILLUSIONMENT

ABOUT A YEAR INTO MY MARRIAGE, I ENTERED THE PhD program at McMaster. Within a few weeks, a familiar old feeling slipped back into my life. I called it fatigue, and blamed myself for not taking a proper summer holiday between my degrees. But I knew that it was depression. I suddenly felt profoundly, inexplicably demoralized. The depression penetrated my body and mind like a flu virus. It was the last thing I had expected, and I desperately hoped it would be temporary. My new classes were about to begin, courses on the great philosopher Georg Hegel and the theologian Dietrich Bonhoeffer, on Vedanta Indian philosophy, and on German and French translation. But I had no energy, no enthusiasm. I was embarrassed by how debilitating the feeling was, and I was determined to mask the effects until it passed.

I forced myself to concentrate and work hard, but my depression got worse. My thoughts became darker, and I found myself easily agitated. The target of my anger was close to home, right inside my own Religious Studies department. Any time another student said anything that sounded even faintly like old-fashioned religious conviction, it set me off. Religious assumptions of any kind began to strike me as unacademic and anti-intellectual. Socially, I was only drawn to the most cynical students in the program. I viewed more and more colleagues as sad wishful thinkers, believing what they wanted to believe, looking to their academic work to defend their faith.

It wasn't that I questioned the existence of God. Atheism, the idea that humans were alone in the universe, still seemed unimaginable to me, and as threatening as the Russian communists of my childhood whom I'd believed, without religion, had no moral compass. Rather, I just didn't think there was anything to say to God. He felt distant and disinterested. He certainly didn't answer our prayers. The world was filled with suffering. So what exactly did we owe him? I was questioning the personal God of my youth in a way I'd never done before. I had finally lost all faith that God had a hand in my birth. It just didn't make sense.

One day, my irritation crossed a line. I sat in a small graduate seminar listening to a presentation by a harmless and soft-spoken fellow student who quoted Plato approvingly. I had come to loathe Plato's influence on Christianity, with his simplistic hierarchy of values, his pyramid of so-called levels of reality where the idea of a thing is more real than the thing itself. Worse was his Gnostic dualism, dividing the world into the few who knew the truth and the many who didn't. And of course the student casually interchanged Christian and Platonic words for *truth* and *God*. His smug assumptions made me want to scream. I fidgeted with frustration while he presented his paper, until I could stand it no longer. I abruptly gathered up my books and stormed out of the class.

Even as I shut the door behind me, I knew I was being disruptive and rude. I was sure the professor would find my hostile gesture disrespectful and disappointing. The earnest fellow student would be confused and embarrassed. But it was too late. I had become an existentialist prima donna. I'd had enough of naive and optimistic people who only believed what they wanted to believe because it made them feel happier, safer, superior. They needed to grow up and face the abyss, like me.

I became captivated by the abstract concept of "nothingness." Standing on the very precipice of despair, I found something that felt like meaning: simply put, the hesitation to jump. And in spite of all this nothingness, I sometimes snuck out on a Sunday morning and attended Mass alone, lonesome and homesick for the way things used to be. And always, I gravitated to my mother's table for Sunday dinner, anxious to please.

⤙

In the same way that sewing clothes throughout high school had cloaked my depression, I now disguised my low spirits with a new distraction. With a loan from my father, Gordon and I bought our very first home. It was a tiny wood frame one-and-a-half-storey 1940s wartime house with blue siding and white trim, and I loved it. When I wasn't reading philosophers and theologians for my doctoral courses, I was fiendishly transforming our little Oakville house into a Victorian country cottage. With maniacal effort, I painted and decorated every room. I trolled garage sales on Saturday mornings for cheap, antique furniture, then stripped off the worn varnish and stained them in golden oak and honey pine. I papered the walls with a Victorian "Wedgewood Blue" print. I sewed cream-coloured cotton eyelet café curtains for the windows and Laura Ashley–print chair pads with ruffled edges. I refinished floors and painted ceilings. I loved my little home. It distracted me from the intense fear that something inside me was dying.

Meanwhile, Gordon was buried in his office job and evening accounting courses, and came home from work amazed and amused by the evidence of my decorating fervour. He was too busy with his own increased responsibilities at work to notice my inner struggle.

I had now lost my confidence in an academic career in religious studies. I was ashamed at how quickly I felt depleted of all ambition, all passion. I was an imposter, having sold myself as a serious and committed doctoral student when I clearly wasn't one. I couldn't keep my personal issues out of the classroom. I convinced myself that the McMaster professors who had supported me with enthusiasm throughout my master's degree were now disillusioned with me.

When Gordon got offered a job at a computer company on the east side of Toronto, it forced a decision. If he took it, we would have to move back to Toronto, and I would be too far from my graduate school to commute. But perhaps what I needed was a fresh start. I formally withdrew from McMaster's Department of Religious Studies and transferred back to York University, into an interdisciplinary graduate program called Social and Political Thought. Instead of religious apologists, the students here were more likely to be Marxists, and that was a relief, because political theory wasn't painfully personal to me in the way religious studies had become.

After starting his new job in a much larger corporate culture, Gordon went from being an exceptionally playful person to someone swallowed up by work worries. His new employers had little appreciation for his irreverent attitude and social eccentricities. His whole life was now consumed by mystifying office politics and a more demanding workload. At school, I made little academic progress. Even a few years in, I was hardly closer to completing my doctoral thesis than when I'd arrived at York. Most of the time, neither Gordon nor I understood or appreciated each other's very separate struggles and fears.

During the ten years of our marriage, we would move residences a total of nine times. Half of every year was dominated by either packing or unpacking. And each new home produced in me a near-frantic decorating phase. Every move seemed rational at the time, a new opportunity, a new beginning, but looking back, each fit a nightmarish pattern of restlessness, an instinctive lunge forward to avoid falling.

⤙

I had stopped addressing my journal entries to the other Gail. The change had been gradual. Looking outside of myself for direction and advice clearly wasn't working. My diary was instead becoming a relentless personal attack, a catalogue of my failings. Gone was my dream of being a great philosopher of the late-twentieth century. I felt I had no future in academics at all. I wasn't smart enough. I wasn't driven or devoted enough. I'd lost my passion and zeal. I was a fraud. And I was letting everyone down. My professors. Gordon. My family. My mother. I played with the word *disappointment* endlessly in my head, doodling on scraps of paper until the words were rendered meaningless and unrecognizable.

Dis-appointment. Dis-appointed. Dis-ap-pointing. What is the point?

One grey and lonely afternoon, while Gordon was at work, I began to read old journals, going back several years; the entries that began "Dear Gail" made me cringe. As I read,

I started to cry. There was so little evidence of any progress in my life. Over and over again, year after year, the pages focused on self-doubt and depression. It seemed no hope, no desire for change, however fervent, ever amounted to anything. Through my tears, I began to rip out the pages from the last few years, one after the other, until I'd destroyed every entry I'd ever addressed to the other Gail. I tore them out at the spine, then tore them again in vertical strips and jumbled them together into an unreadable heap. I hid the strips in an old paper bag and buried them deep inside the garbage bin.

I had completed my course requirements and began working mostly from home, researching for my comprehensive exams. For my dissertation, I had settled on an early Enlightenment philosopher, Baruch Spinoza. What interested me most was a non-religious, non-authoritarian, rational basis for human morality. But the more time I spent in the house, alone with my thoughts and recriminations all day while Gordon was at work, the more isolated I became. I tried to keep my dark state of mind a secret, from him, but especially from my mother. I came to hate going outside, even for groceries. I was no longer able to make eye contact with the cashier in the store around the corner from my house.

During this troubled period, I became convinced that it was time for Gordon and I to start a family. I was nearly twenty-seven years old, after all, and my friends were having children. Gordon agreed. Six months went by. I began to take my body temperature with a basal thermometer first thing every morning before I got out of bed, and recorded it on a monthly chart, looking for signs of ovulation. A year went by.

Then Gordon came home from work with news that he was being offered a job transfer to Ottawa. We didn't agonize for long. My academic progress had ground to a halt. Maybe I needed a radical change of scenery, a sabbatical, to refresh myself. I applied to take a leave of absence from York's doctoral program.

While Gordon was in Ottawa for a business meeting in the days before we moved, I went to a party with a few fellow York grad students. For the first time in my life, I got drunk. Fall-down drunk. Two kind friends pulled me up from the floor and saw me safely home. I had been celebrating, the way you do at an Irish wake. The students I'd met during those few years at York had been the best part of my experience there, and I was going to miss them.

Within a month of moving to Ottawa, I withdrew from my academic program entirely. I'd lost all faith that I could ever recover the enthusiasm I'd once had, that drive that had helped me excel in the past. I was no longer good enough, special enough, to succeed in the competitive world of scholarship. I was ashamed of myself, but I also felt relieved. "Withdrawn in good standing" is what my graduate record would state. Technically, I could go back to complete my PhD dissertation within ten years; at the time, that's what I told myself I would do. I never did.

⤙

One Sunday afternoon just before the move to Ottawa, I'd sat slouched at my mother's kitchen table. She was standing at the sink, her back to me. We were alone.

Suddenly, hesitantly, she said, "Sometimes I think I made a mistake naming you Gail."

Many years later, I came to realize that my mother might have been trying to say something very different on that day, but I was unable to hear it. Instead, I heard her questioning whether I should have been named Gail because I'd failed to live up to the name.

I felt nothing but the impact of her words. *She would take my name away from me if she could.* There was chaos in my head, like a seizure robbing me of my faculties. Mercifully, as if the pounding of my heart had alarmed her, she changed the subject quickly. But my panic lingered.

All of my siblings had their own names and their own lives to live, but not me. My life had one purpose, to be the other Gail, to be the Gail that *she* would have been, *should* have been, if only she hadn't died. I was nothing if I was not named Gail. I was no one if I was not the other Gail in my mother's eyes. She might as well have said she regretted that I'd ever been born, given how I'd turned out.

And that's when it hit me. My whole life, my dead sister had been known as the "other Gail," but all along, *I* was the "other Gail." She was the *real* Gail. I was just the replacement. I was the changeling. I was the "other."

I hadn't been able to live up to the perfect innocence of an infant angel. No one knew that better than me. But I wondered about my mother. Had my failure caused her to doubt her miracle? Of all my hellish horrors, this was the most unthinkable, that I might tear from her the belief that God had given her precious baby back to her. That I might reawaken all that grief, her baby left for dead after all.

PART 4

22

APOCALYPSE

IN OTTAWA, WE BOUGHT ANOTHER WOOD-FRAME house, this one with four small bedrooms, the kind built for a growing family in the 1930s. I imagined children's voices, their scampering feet in the rooms upstairs as I worked with a putty knife, scraping off the faded floral paper on the kitchen's plaster walls. I wanted my own baby very badly. I had now been trying to get pregnant for eighteen months. It was painful to get my old school friends' birth announcements in the mail, one sweet baby picture after another.

After we'd been settling in for a month or so, my mother called to say she and my father were driving up to Ottawa for a visit. Gordon must have spoken to her about me—about how low I'd been—because she asked how I was and sounded concerned when I said I was fine.

They stayed for the weekend. We had no heart-to-heart talk. We spoke of nothing personal at all. But I felt her anxious charcoal eyes following me through the house as I discussed my renovation projects and decorating schemes. I feared that I looked pale and fragile and weak, and I didn't want her to notice. Everyone else in the family might see me that way, but I didn't want her to. I didn't want to be that person.

Her visit marked a turning point. It raised in me a powerful desire to buck up and pull myself together. After they left, I admonished myself for wallowing in so much sadness and self-pity. It wasn't only pointless, it was irresponsible. Even morally reprehensible. I told myself that to hold together, to stay strong and rational and functional, was a duty. It was *my duty*.

I tried to address my fears of failure head-on. No, I would never be a saint or great philosopher. I needed to accept that. I needed the courage to be nobody.

I began to look for a job. I made a list of places that interested me and sent out copies of my resumé. I soon got a call back from a CBC Radio program on religion and ethics called *Open House* that was produced out of Ottawa. When I met with the executive producer, she asked if there were any specific topics in religion that interested me. I talked about the act of confession, the way it was equally interesting both in the Catholic tradition and in human psychology generally. Don't we all long to confess? To be forgiven? I walked out with a modest contract and a portable tape recorder on loan.

A few months later, I stood in my mother's kitchen on a weekend visit to Toronto, the radio tuned in to the CBC, as my eight-minute documentary on confession began to play. I had written and narrated it, and had interviewed a few religion experts for the piece. I was excited and nervous to have my mother hear it. The documentary praised the virtue and wisdom of one of the Catholic Church's prized holy sacraments, so she could hardly disapprove, could she? When I saw her eyes light up and mouth open in surprise at my voice on national radio, I was overjoyed. She was proud of me again. It felt like redemption.

I was now working for the weekly radio show as a full-time researcher. It was a perfect fit. *Open House* covered a wide range of topics, from the most conventional religious views to the most unconventional. I learned to prepare effectively, to ask the right questions and to listen well. One of my first assignments was to produce an interview about Pope John Paul II's latest papal encyclical on liberation theology, in response to Latin American priests becoming social activists. I enjoyed wading through dense theological and ecclesiastical language and translating it into something that a lay audience could follow. I was confident that there was no idea too difficult for most people to understand. It was only the language used that made it seem so. The goal was to be accessible. I felt my skills and education finally had a practical application.

I also learned how to hide my opinion from the people I interviewed in order to get them to open up. I was a chameleon.

I remember pre-interviewing a notoriously conservative Catholic theologian about a controversial topic in preparation for her appearance on the show. At the end of our phone call, she asked me if I was Catholic. I told her that, as a matter of fact, I was. She said she had strongly suspected as much.

"You must be a very *good* Catholic," she added.

In truth, I had personally disagreed with everything she'd said, but she'd never guessed. It was satisfying to put my natural-born talent as an imposter to such constructive use.

Over the next six months, I engaged in religious and ethical issues with a pleasure I'd never experienced in academics. Radio journalists were intelligent, but they were also fun. I enjoyed our lively brainstorming meetings. I got to talk to important authors and activists and religious leaders. All the while, I kept my mother up to date on my adventures with weekly phone calls. She listened, captivated, as I told her about pre-interviewing famous people on profound subjects.

⌁

But there was a painful side to my life: my failure to become pregnant. I began treatment at a fertility clinic, taking powerful fertility drugs, getting monthly ultrasounds and undergoing rounds of artificial insemination. The hormonal injections produced a chaos of emotions, with each month ending in a devastating crash. What else was menstruation but the blood of my dead baby? Every period brought with it a week of acute depression.

Finally, after a few months of failure, I told Gordon I couldn't handle the monthly ordeal any longer, and we quit the program. Later that week, I sent away for information on international adoptions. When I told my mother the news over the phone, she announced that she was going to say a novena for me. A novena is a repetition of specific prayers to the Blessed Virgin Mary over the course of nine days.

The next month, I found out I was pregnant. I was flabbergasted. When I broke the news to my mother, she reminded me of her novena. Privately, I saw it as a coincidence, but I was happy to have her believe otherwise. The novena certainly hadn't hurt.

Within two months, while I was in the throes of morning sickness, Gordon found out that his position in Ottawa was being terminated and he was being transferred back to Toronto. The timing was terrible. I didn't want to leave my wonderful job. He didn't want to leave his either, but it seemed we had no choice. We would have to move again. Over Christmas, we bought a big house that was still under construction in a new development in Aurora, a town north of Toronto. But construction work fell behind schedule and, in my second trimester of pregnancy, when the time came to leave Ottawa, we had nowhere to live. My mother invited us to move back home until our new house was ready. With only their sons at home by this point, my parents had bedrooms to spare.

At five months pregnant, thanks to the stress of moving and my morning sickness, I weighed less than before I got pregnant. But my mother soon took charge, making breakfast each morning and hot dinners every night. I felt tremendously nurtured, and my pregnancy proceeded smoothly.

During my adolescence, I'd been convinced that my parents hated each other. Now, that no longer seemed to be the case. They had negotiated something close to peace. My father seemed more contented. He was no longer managing the service station that had given him so much grief while his seven children were growing up. He was now working as a simple auto mechanic, and had reasonable hours and no managerial headaches. The battles between him and my mother over his excessive weekend drinking had declined. He was more careful; she was less angry.

My mother was still reserved, but there was a gentleness in her eyes that I hadn't seen before. Maybe it was an effect of becoming a grandmother. She had half a dozen grandchildren now—Linda and Glenna both had sons, and Melanie had daughters—and they brought a new pleasure to her life.

But it was more than that. She had begun to work part-time, first as a supply teacher and then for the Sears catalogue store. She told me that going back to work had been good for her confidence. She said she'd always suffered from anxiety but had tried to hide it from others. She now believed that during her thirties, she'd been suffering from a kind of mental illness—she'd been trying to raise her large family in the midst of a terrible amount of psychological distress.

"Many times through those years, I felt half insane," she said.

In spite of the many times I'd written in my teenage diary that she was raving mad, her confession surprised me. She had always seemed so in control, of herself and everyone around her. She had always been the most formidable person I knew. I wondered if this was an acknowledgement that she'd been emotionally abusive toward me during my teen years. I listened sympathetically, but I didn't ask what she thought was behind her mental suffering, and she didn't offer an explanation. Was it her father's drinking? The early death of her mother? Her traumatic adolescence? Or was it the car accident and death of the other Gail?

There was a silence between us that kept us from getting too close, a space that I couldn't bear to enter for fear of losing myself.

⌁

By the time Gordon and I could finally move into our newly constructed house in Aurora, our baby was nearly due. It was a difficult delivery but he was healthy. In fact, he was beautiful. He was perfect. He was adorable. We named him Benjamin.

But as much as I loved my son, staying home alone all day in this barren new development miles north of Toronto was difficult. Gordon worked long hours at the office and I rarely saw or spoke to anyone while he was gone. To make matters worse, we were worried about money. I began searching the town's thin weekly paper for part-time jobs. I applied for a small writing contract, without success. Then, when Ben was barely four months old, I got a phone call from the executive producer of the prestigious CBC Radio show *Morningside*. They had a sudden hole to fill—a producer they'd only just hired had quit without notice—and she wanted to know if I could come in to produce stories for them for two weeks. I was practically trembling with nervous excitement. I knew *Morningside*: it was a three-hour national show that was broadcast live every weekday morning, and was hosted by CBC Radio icon Peter Gzowski.

I couldn't believe I had a chance to work for *Morningside*, however briefly, with so little experience as a radio producer. But I worried about whether Ben was old enough to be left with a babysitter, and whether I was ready to leave him with one. I felt sick with anxiety at the thought of our separation, which would be made even longer by the gruelling commute into downtown Toronto. But I was afraid to pass up this rare opportunity. I told myself that with a kind-hearted and responsible babysitter on weekdays, and my full attention on evenings and weekends, his life would still be good.

↓

The CBC Radio building was a four-floor brownstone walk-up that had been converted, only just barely, from a rambling century-old private girls school. The building seemed designed to withstand an earthquake. The halls were wide, the staircases massive and made of stone, the walls thick and the windows opaque. Offices were large and open, filled with desks cluttered with papers and books, mechanical typewriters and phones. There was the unmistakable feel of a prestigious old institution that had been overrun by squatters—squatters who were brilliant, dedicated and idealistic. And since this was still the 1980s, some who fit the image of hard-drinking, chain-smoking journalists. The veteran producers I met were awe-inspiring and intimidating. Each morning, after that day's broadcast, we stood at our desks in the large open office and, one at a time, pitched story ideas to Gzowski and the rest of the unit for the following day's show. Taking my turn tested my nerves like few things I'd ever done before.

Working at *Morningside* was the best of times and the worst of times. It felt like the centre of the world. I had never known such exhilaration or dread, often on the same day.

Gzowski was the show's editorial compass, a large, restless man in perpetual motion, pacing, chain-smoking, peering at you inscrutably from above the rims of his reading glasses. Tall and hunched, with greying head and beard, he always looked slightly dishevelled and exhausted from his 5 a.m. wake-up calls. He was warm and friendly on the radio, but in person he was introverted and often irritable. He was ruthlessly demanding of quality work and he could be dismissive and outright mean to producers he didn't think could cut it. We vied for his approval because his judgment of good radio was without parallel.

We wrestled with the big questions, whether of ordinary people in small towns or on the international stage. We interviewed politicians, celebrities, world-class thinkers, makers of strawberry jam and quilts and canoes, writers, actors, singers and performers of every kind. No one in the country would turn down an invitation to be interviewed by Peter Gzowski on *Morningside*. My initial two-week contract was extended through the winter and then through to the end of the season in June.

My mother was deeply impressed. She listened with pride and interest to all of my stories, anecdotes and gossip. But my own feelings were ambivalent. Outside office hours, I felt overwhelmed, exhausted, plagued by tension headaches and insomnia, and so pained by separation from my son that I often cried as I drove my car north on the highway at the end of the day, weeping at the thought of him waiting for me at the babysitter's.

Tensions with Gordon were steadily building too. He was already finding his new job very stressful, and fatherhood had awakened additional anxieties. He had no positive role model; his own father was an alcoholic who'd died when Gordon was fourteen. Now that I was working again, and working such long hours, pressures were even more burdensome. While my job at least kept me pumped with adrenalin, Gordon was getting much less gratification from his, and he felt the hours I worked weren't fair to him or to our son.

At the *Morningside* office, I felt different from everyone else, unsophisticated and old-fashioned, like I'd just arrived in the big city from a very small town, or worse, from another era. More than once, a producer swore and then turned to me to apologize. When we had our office Christmas party, everyone bought gag gifts for a Secret Santa exchange. I'd pulled the name of the studio director, Charlie, a painfully introverted man with a reputation for his sharp intelligence and encyclopedic knowledge. I bought him a Ouija board. Every gift brought laughter and amusement, until it came to the one with my name on it. I opened the little box to find a fragile miniature china vase wrapped in tissue, the one unfunny gift of the lot. My Secret Santa revealed herself to me, explaining somewhat apologetically that she'd thought the little vase somehow suited me. I was embarrassed, fearing that everyone there found me hopelessly square, like some kind of fragile, middle-aged church lady.

I hadn't gotten to know anyone well at *Morningside* in that first season. People were friendly, but I didn't have the time or energy to socialize. And I couldn't relate to my colleagues anyway, so worldly and hip compared to me. One day, a co-worker named Alex told me I had a "holy" expression on my face when I walked into the office each morning, like I was seeing a vision. He knew nothing about me. Was my secret past somehow bleeding through?

Another time, I was sitting at a desk beside a producer who was on loan from one of the more news-focused shows. We struck up a conversation, briefly discussing some potential story for the next day's show that included a reference to reincarnation. I jokingly shared with him my belief that I might have been reincarnated. He immediately wanted to know more. It felt like such a long time since I'd spoken of it, but I quickly told him the story of my dead baby sister, my labour-free birth, my mother's conviction that I'd been brought back from the dead through her prayers. I spoke casually, like it was no big deal. But I saw his eyes widen. He leaned in, saying that it must have been hard, growing up under that kind of pressure. I shrugged. "Not really," I said, and immediately felt embarrassed. Why had I volunteered something so sensitive and private to a near stranger?

At the end of the season, the executive producer gave me a job review that boosted my confidence in my work and assured me a place on the show for the next season. I was able to take the summer off, and I relished the time spent with Ben, who was now almost a year old. But once I was away from the office, I shuddered at the memory of the long hours and pressure I'd endured. I dreaded going back to face the madness again in September. I managed to convince Gordon that at least we should sell our big suburban house and move closer to Toronto to cut down on travel time.

Meanwhile, my mother's pride in me was soaring. She and my father had driven down to PEI for their annual summer vacation, and she'd come home flush with the realization that our down-east relatives were huge fans of *Morningside*. Linda mentioned that my mother was always bragging about me; she said, only half joking, that it could be quite nauseating. My mother still gave so little praise to my face—I had to read in her eyes that she was proud of me, and those subtle cues still meant as much as ever.

⤙

Gordon and I had gone through the first eight years of our marriage each focused on our own dramatically different work lives, but there was rarely any outward conflict when we were together at home. We never fought. My years of anxiety and depression hadn't come between us, partly because I kept as much as I could to myself, and perhaps too because he had indulged my moodiness as a natural part of what he'd once called my "Annie Hall" character. Now, things were changing. We became brittle and unsympathetic around each other. We barely talked anymore, except to argue about our conflicting schedules. Neither of us had any energy to spare for the other's emotional problems.

It was only a month into my second season at *Morningside* when I found myself unable to cope. I made an appointment with an employment counsellor to talk about my desire to change jobs. I sat hunched over in his office, staring down, hands shaking, describing the pressure of my job, the long hours, the strain on my marriage, and the negative impact on my health and sanity. He asked me why, in that case, I was hesitating to leave. What was the problem? I broke down and began crying so hard that I could barely speak the words.

"I don't want to disappoint my mother."

He gently pushed me to explain. I left his office an hour later with the name and number of a psychiatrist. It turned out that an employment counsellor wasn't what I needed after all.

23

EXORCISM

All my life, you have been my dead sister. They named me after you. I am so much like you, if you'd been born later, they'd have named you after me. But you are more real than I have ever been. Admit it. You are Gail. I am only the other Gail.

❧

I began to see a psychiatrist. For the first time ever, I started to really think about the role the other Gail had played in my life. The circumstances of my birth had always made me feel special. At the same time, though, I felt as if I had to do something special to deserve this miracle. I had to make up for the family tragedy. Pay the debt.

I began to see the other Gail as the fundamental problem of my life. She had taken possession of me since birth. Now I wanted her gone, but I still couldn't imagine myself without her. It was as though the only thing worse than being the other Gail all my life was not being her after all.

The early sessions were eviscerating, like lancing a boil. I'd spent my whole life trying to be someone else, trying to make my mother happy, trying to ease her pain. Anger filled me until I was choking. The psychiatrist recommended a long-term commitment to treatment. I started taking antidepressants and Xanax.

This is when I began to fantasize daily about being punched in the face, or having a knife plunged into my chest. On the highway, when I drove home from work, I saw every concrete support holding up an overpass as a kind of invitation. Each was a solid white door into another dimension, beckoning me to come inside. I imagined the beauty of the sudden compression.

For many months I hid my darker thoughts from everyone close to me—my husband, my friends and colleagues, my mother. Gordon had too many things on his mind to even ask about my therapy sessions. But my mother suspected something was wrong. She thought my face was very pale. She suggested I wear more blush, though she didn't want me to take the suggestion personally.

"I've never met a woman who had enough natural colour in her cheeks," she said, as if a deficiency of blush had been Eve's second and lesser-known original sin.

At work, I thought my makeup looked just fine. No one

would ever guess what I was hiding. But the darkness building inside me was overwhelming. I didn't know how much longer I could contain it.

I was at my second *Morningside* Christmas party, at Peter Gzowski's cottage. I'd had a few drinks and was struggling to keep composed. Gzowski's executive assistant, ever observant, noticed that I was in distress. She pulled me into a bedroom and we sat on the edge of the bed to talk. She wanted to know what was wrong. When I started crying, she put her arm around me. "Why are you so unhappy?" she asked. I couldn't put it into words, but I admitted that she was right. For the very first time, I had confessed my deep despair to a friend. It was a momentous breakthrough.

After that Christmas party, I began to socialize more at work. It felt good to get caught up in my co-workers' lives, share in their dramas. I was making new friends.

⤙

I'd always had bad menstrual pain, but I'd attributed it to nature or neurosis, something I just had to live with. Except it kept getting worse, and finally an ultrasound showed a large growth engulfing my right ovary. I worried that it was cancer. Instead, it turned out to be advanced endometriosis, and my ovary had to be removed.

Gordon didn't need the extra pressure caused by my health scare. His mother had recently had a massive heart attack, and now this. As I recuperated from major surgery, I was anxious to see Ben, but I had to urge an exhausted Gordon to bring our son to the hospital during the evening visiting hours.

Several of my co-workers visited me, and the *Morningside* office sent flowers to the hospital. Someone sent a very large arrangement separately, signed "*le directeur.*" It took me a couple of days to figure out that the mystery flowers were from the studio director, Charlie, for whom I'd bought the Ouija board at a past Christmas party. Once I was home, my long abdominal scar healing badly, I phoned Charlie to thank him. He invited me for lunch the following week at a restaurant near the house he shared with his long-time partner, and I accepted. We discussed T.S. Eliot, and then he invited me back to his place for a coffee and to show me some of his own poems. I didn't stay long. He seemed as deep and dark as anyone I'd ever met, like the saddest, most introverted, most anxious person in the world. I felt sorry for him, but his furtiveness also made being alone with him uncomfortable.

When I returned to work after my surgery, there was a present on my desk. It was a book from Charlie, *The Crying of Lot 49* by Thomas Pynchon. He had written on the inside cover, "We are all in this together." I didn't care for the attention but I thanked him politely. I read the book, a strange postmodern conspiracy story, paranoid and funny. Meanwhile, I tried to avoid running into Charlie in the office because I didn't want to encourage him further. The brief moments we crossed paths were awkwardly charged.

A week later, Charlie walked out of the *Morningside* studio in the middle of directing a live show. He got on a plane to Manitoba, and holed up at his parents' cottage on Lake Winnipeg. It was still cold, early spring, and cottage country was desolate. I found out later that everyone, including his partner, feared he was having a nervous breakdown. Then, a few days later, I got a very short phone call from Charlie, from a phone booth.

"I was wondering if you would consider running away with me to Argentina?" he asked.

It took me so by surprise that I laughed out loud. He hung up.

A friend of his asked to speak to me privately. He told me he'd received a letter in the mail, and Charlie's partner had too. Charlie was now on the record—he'd left Toronto because he couldn't stand to work with me there. It was too painful. I was embarrassed, and somewhat defensive. No, I had not done anything to cause this.

The word spread. How could it not? It was such a good story. I defended myself to Gzowski, who was upset that his brilliant studio director had gone AWOL, presumably because of me. He wanted to know what had really happened.

"Absolutely nothing happened between us," I said. "All we did was discuss poetry."

Gzowski rolled his eyes.

"Poor guy," he said.

I had more important things to worry about. I had no emotional energy to spend on Charlie's pain or theatrics. I hardly knew him, and wanted to keep it that way. It was embarrassing to know I was the subject of gossip, but I was determined to let it blow over, and it would, for a time.

⤙

Shortly after the Charlie incident I was presented with a job offer in CBC Television, as a researcher for a documentary series called *Man Alive*. Television meant a higher public profile, and *Man Alive* focused on spiritual and ethical topics. In other words, this was news I could happily share with my mother. I was relieved, too, because my new hours were nine to five, with none of the daily pressure of a live radio show. I accepted right away, and felt hopeful for the first time in a while.

A few months later, Gordon and I had a heart-to-heart talk. I confessed that I thought our marriage was in trouble. I felt emotionally fractured and vulnerable. I had developed a crush on a co-worker, a writer who'd been on a short-term contract with *Morningside*. He had a gentle manner and a self-deprecating sense of humour. He had also been raised in a devout Irish-Catholic family and did a wickedly funny Irish priest impersonation. I felt a strong connection with him. He had moved on by the time Gordon and I had our talk, but I knew my infatuation had been a bad sign. We would need to make a drastic change to salvage our marriage.

Gordon seemed remarkably calm, even philosophical about my disclosure. But he surprised me by arriving home from work the next day with the news that he'd just quit the job that had been making him so miserable. He wanted to go back to university, to change careers completely. He was thinking about social work. I was surprised, but at this point, it seemed to me that any change would be for the better.

We sold our latest house in north Toronto after only a year, and moved, one last time, into an apartment down in the Toronto Beaches. We would rent, and Gordon would begin university classes in September.

⤝

As a researcher and then associate producer on *Man Alive*, I worked with a wonderfully diverse mix of directors. The documentaries we produced on spirituality, social ethics, moral dilemmas, heroes and victims were intellectually engaging and creatively challenging. I was learning so much about making television, and the subject matter was a perfect fit. It gave me more interesting stories to share with my mother.

But privately, I felt no less disturbed and depressed, ragged from my weekly psychiatric sessions, emotions whirling. The feeling of estrangement from Gordon only grew. Each day, I spent my commute on the Queen Street streetcar writing notes, fragments of thoughts and poetry, full of religious imagery, dark and desperate and magical. *Some say death is black, but I'm quite sure it's white.*

One day, a tiny elderly lady got on the streetcar at Leslie Street and made her way down the aisle toward me, smiling graciously and murmuring thanks to those who offered her their seat, but saying she was getting off soon. She had a sweet voice. She stood very close to where I sat, near the back doors, and watched for her stop, still smiling, though now at no one in particular. Her small, wrinkled face emitted a celestial radiance, both ancient and new. It struck me with a great force that she was an angel. I couldn't look away from her, and when she alit from the back door steps, I strained to see whether her feet were touching the sidewalk.

The thought of an elderly angel thrilled me. An old and fragile spirit, burning bright. She was like a sign of hope from heaven. *Angels live and die and live and die and live again.* Death and resurrection, everywhere I looked.

I began to imagine the presence of the Blessed Virgin Mary all along the Queen Street East route. Running her finger through the plastic flags marking the boundaries of the used car lot. Blowing kisses to the hot dog–eating boy on the billboard sign. Mother Mary standing in the window of the St. Michael's Hospital foyer, drinking coffee from a paper cup. *I am living in a wonderland of ghosts*, I wrote. Angels and ghosts.

The following spring, Gordon and I sat on separate couches in a large office, the marital therapist facing us from the other side of the room. I felt unbearably tense and irritable. Gordon accused me of not wanting to save our marriage. I realized he was right. I had already lost all faith. I felt too emotionally distant from Gordon to ever recover, and postponing our inevitable end served no other purpose than to prolong our suffering.

That evening, I admitted to Gordon that I didn't think it was possible to salvage what we once had. He didn't fight, he didn't argue, but he was crushed, and profoundly saddened. Within weeks, he moved out and into an apartment nearby. He got the car, I got the furniture.

Earlier that year, while he was attending university and pursuing a degree in social work, he had joined a men's support group. It became a lifeline for him. He would meet his second wife while working for mental health services after graduating. Eventually, he would return to the computer industry, not in management but as a software technician. He would finally find his niche.

Whatever disapproval my family felt about the breakup, they kept it mostly to themselves. I knew they felt very bad for Gordon. A few old friends commented that they thought he'd always "kept my feet on the ground" with his common sense approach to life, and I could tell they worried that now I'd be even less stable. But my mother accepted the news with a calmness, even a kindness, that made me feel she understood me better than I'd realized.

Divorce was a terrible stigma for Catholics, but for better or worse, Glenna had already broken the ice in our family with an acrimonious divorce. Next to it, my divorce from Gordon was more like a handshake. We wrote up our own separation agreement without conflict and we divorced without lawyers. I moved with Ben into a new home nearby with a more affordable rent. Ben visited his dad twice a week, and spent alternating weekends with him as he got older.

I enjoyed my new life as a single mother. I felt a tremendous freedom and relief. I loved having more emotional energy to focus on Ben, and our home felt peaceful and cozy. I quit my psychiatrist and set about weaning myself off of antidepressants. I had run out of things to say about my past. I had finally exorcised my ghost. Or so I thought.

Ben's babysitter described him as happy and active, but she also said he was different.

"Often he's so concentrated on what he's doing that he tunes me and the other children completely out," she said. "He plays in his own little world."

She used the term *parallel play*. I had never heard it before and it stuck with me. She said, "He sits, surrounded by other children of a similar age all playing a board game together, while he makes spiderwebs out of my knitting yarn. For hours at a time, connecting the furniture in complex patterns. One of these days I'm going to trip over one of his creations and break my neck."

I was always impressed by the way Ben focused so intently on his Lego blocks, building complex, perfectly symmetrical structures, or by how he would amuse himself for hours with a garden hose and a patch of mud. Our backyard looked like a miniature irrigation system. I was sure our neighbours were horrified at the sight of his earthworks where there used to be a landscaped garden. True, Ben wasn't engaging directly with other children his age, but he seemed so content. I was proud of his little projects, his amazing concentration, his creativity, and I assumed they were genetic. Gordon's mother said that Gordon had played in the same focused way when he was a child. In his own little world.

Ben's first round of psychological testing began when he was three and a half years old. Early results were inconclusive. The team assessing him recommended that Gordon and I both seek personal support. They enrolled Gordon in a parenting program at the hospital, and they recommended I consider more psychotherapy to deal with my anxiety. It was a blow, and felt like a setback, but I began seeing a psychiatrist again. This one was a former child psychiatrist with a Roman Catholic background, so he seemed a good fit.

It wasn't until Ben started school that his eccentricities began to cause him problems. He wasn't doing any work during class; it was as though he was neurologically unable to cope in that setting. When he was seven, extensive cognitive testing revealed a score in the superior intelligence range, with a vocabulary and logical reasoning four years beyond his age. But he was placed in a self-contained special-education stream for children with learning disabilities. It was only when Ben was a young teen that a child psychiatrist would finally, officially, place him on the autism spectrum, diagnosing Asperger's syndrome.

I had long noticed some similar patterns in father and son, but Gordon was the first to raise the topic openly, acknowledging that he could identify aspects of Asperger's in himself. Talking to psychologists and psychiatrists about high-functioning Autism Spectrum Disorder helped to illuminate at least some of the dynamics of our marriage, but it was too late to make a difference.

24

DESCENT

ONE OF MY *MORNINGSIDE* FRIENDS CALLED AND INVITED me to join the old radio gang for drinks after work. They were going to meet at a pub on Bloor Street. I was feeling particularly lonely that day and thought perhaps this was just what I needed. I arranged for Ben to stay with Gordon overnight.

When I arrived at the pub, I found the table of *Morningside* producers, and sitting among them was Charlie, looking as self-conscious as ever. I was taken aback. I'd never seen him at an after-work get-together before. I worked in a different CBC building now, and I'd managed to avoid him completely since his return to *Morningside* many months before. I immediately felt ambushed.

Charlie smiled and greeted me. I asked him how he was and he was quick to tell me that he'd separated from his long-time partner and was now sexually involved with a woman who lived upstairs from his new apartment. The information came out fast and unsolicited. It was as if he was anxious to say he was no longer pining for me.

"He just wants to say goodbye," my friend whispered. "He says this is the last time he will ever try to see you."

I felt I was being asked to be kind. Apparently he was talking about moving out west. If this really was the last time I'd lay eyes on Charlie, that was absolutely fine with me.

Someone ordered B-52 shots, and the waiter held the tray out to me. I'd never had one before. It slipped down. Charlie handed me a small piece of paper, a short poem scribbled in pen. The poem was called "My Plan" and ended with the lines,

When you are no longer the most beautiful woman in
 the world,
you'll need me and you'll call. I'll wait for that.
It's better than no plan at all.

It didn't sound like goodbye. I was mildly flattered. Who doesn't want to be an object of desire? But then I became deeply depressed. Not his desire. Not him. More B-52s appeared. I had another. I was trying to be sociable. Everything started feeling more tragic by the minute. I left the table, looked for the washroom, and found it downstairs. I was very dizzy. When I came out of the washroom, I was grabbed and kissed hard on the mouth. It was Charlie. He had followed me downstairs and had waited outside the washroom for me. Waited to surprise me with a kiss. Here in the basement, with no one else around.

I pulled away. *Jerk*, I thought. I made my way upstairs, unsteadily, as though nothing had happened. He followed behind me, whether sheepishly or triumphantly, I don't know. I was pretty drunk.

The gathering eventually moved on to someone's apartment. I don't remember exactly how the evening ended. I only know that I woke up the next morning in a single bed in the spare bedroom with Charlie lying beside me. We were both fully clothed. I was sure that we hadn't had sex, and I had no memory of kissing him, but in that single bed there had at least been some type of physical embrace. I was overcome by a toxic wave of guilt. Worrying what others would assume triggered in me a deep-seated fear of sexual impropriety.

Neither Charlie nor I spoke. He left quickly, rushing to make his 6 a.m. start time in the studio. I stumbled out later, hungover and mortified. I vowed I would never drink like that again.

Late that morning, Charlie phoned me at work, insisting he needed to see me at lunch, that we needed to talk. I didn't want to, but there was such urgency in his voice. I feared I had unintentionally led him on. I had to apologize, and to set him straight.

I never got a chance. I couldn't get a word in before Charlie began talking non-stop. He drove me to High Park, where, for the next hour, he overwhelmed me with a diatribe of intellectual and poetic arguments as to why I should, at the very least, "give him a chance." He drew on the verbal skills of his unused law degree and every ounce of his substantial mental muscle to present an irrefutable case.

"There is a profound connection between us," he said. "A once-in-a-lifetime gift, and we shouldn't ignore it. We shouldn't pass it up without even testing it."

I didn't feel a positive connection with Charlie—only a shared propensity for anxiety and depression and alienation, the very things I hated most about myself. And yet, his words touched a nerve. Perhaps it was a long-buried memory of the chance not taken with Matthew so many years before. What if Charlie was right? My life had been marked by fear of risk, fear of chaos, fear of being different. Fear, fear, fear. Charlie and I were so different that, if nothing else, dating him would be counterintuitive, rebellious even, an act in pure defiance of other people's expectations.

"I'm just asking you to give us a few months. You have nothing to lose," he said. "If it doesn't work out, if you aren't happy with me, I can guarantee you I will be easy to get rid of."

Those were the lines that would prove the most persuasive, and the least accurate. He made me promise to think about it. Then he drove me back to work and left me reeling on the sidewalk. I had barely uttered a word. My brain felt pulverized.

I worried about my reputation—the potentially embarrassing gossip that I'd led on a fragile, vulnerable man, and that everyone who knew us would think that I was somehow to blame for Charlie's heartache. As though I'd capriciously stolen his heart. When he spoke about his earlier breakdown and his breakup with his long-time partner, he made me feel that I had derailed his former perfectly stable life.

I felt there was only one honourable way to handle this crushing feeling of guilt and embarrassment: I would give us a chance. I would date Charlie. And turn my unintended indiscretion into an intentional act. Like trying to cover up an awkward stumble with a vaudeville dance move.

In retrospect, I realize that my empathy for his social alienation and my anxiety about moral judgment were Charlie's most powerful advantages over me. But an old friend of his would put it more simply: "He just wore you down." It never occurred to me at the time that, between the two of us, I was the more vulnerable.

✤

It was hard to get used to Charlie's social manner. He was painfully self-conscious around most other people, the kind of person who looked uncomfortable in his own skin. He was fidgety, a nail-biter who compulsively twirled his fingers in his full beard. He could look so shifty-eyed that when a co-worker saw him lingering outside my empty *Man Alive* office one day, she feared he was a thief who had come in off the street.

When we first began dating, I didn't feel attracted to him. But it wasn't long before he grew on me, and I began to see him in a more romanticized light. He was something of a minor legend in the CBC Radio building, known for his intelligence and his vast general knowledge, and I was attracted to the idea of his superior wisdom. I would soon become seduced by his image of himself, and I began to feel flattered that he thought I was worthy of his company.

When it came to thoughts on human nature, Charlie was the most cynical person I'd ever met. Only a choice few of his old friends were exempt from his harsh judgments. He and I, however, were "soul mates," bound by our mutual melancholia and acute understanding of the fundamental tragedy of life. He said my struggle with depression and anxiety was a sign of deeper awareness and sensitivity. It was something I should accept and value. He saw his own suffering as the price paid for his higher consciousness of the human condition. Perhaps, as he suggested, he was a man of such deep sensitivities and painful insight that he was doomed to be an outsider, as though being an out-sider was his proof. I tried to resist the way he twisted our mutual weaknesses into strengths, but I asked myself if I simply lacked his courage—to accept my true self the way he accepted his true self.

Our first real "coming out" as a couple was at a weekend charity golf tournament hosted by Peter Gzowski on the shores of Lake Simcoe. There would be a full evening of entertainment featuring celebrities in comedy routines and musical performances, as well as a reception that all of my old radio co-workers were going to attend. I was really looking forward to it. Charlie and I booked a nearby cabin for the night so we could party without having to make the long drive home afterwards.

From the moment we arrived at the crowded venue, I could tell Charlie wasn't in the mood. He was sullen and withdrawn. He wanted to sit at the back of the auditorium, away from people we knew, and at the show's intermission, he asked if we could go check out our cabin. I wasn't pleased.

"I don't want to miss anything," I said.

"It's predictable stuff."

"But I'm enjoying it."

We arrived at the cabin. The space was small and rustic, with a brass four-poster bed covered with a patchwork quilt. He lay down on the bed as if to check the mattress, and then put his hands behind his head on the pillow. He wanted to have sex. I stood away from him and tried to control my irritation.

"Are you serious?" I felt my voice rising. "I want to go back and watch the rest of the show! I want to hang out with everybody at the reception afterwards!"

He just lay there, not moving. His face became a mask of disappointment, his eyes far away. There was a long silence, and tension filled the room.

"I didn't come all this way, driving an hour north of the city through heavy, end-of-week traffic, just to spend a night in a cabin. It wasn't easy arranging for Gordon to take care of Ben overnight, and I was really in the mood to socialize with my old radio friends."

What I didn't say is how much I wanted to normalize my relationship with Charlie, to show everyone that we were a perfectly happy and ordinary couple. We fit right in. So much for that.

"We can have sex later tonight," I said. "Or in the morning."

That's when he burst out crying, so suddenly, so dramatically, that I was completely startled. He began repeating a lamentation between sobs, as if he was talking to himself.

"This isn't going to work," he was saying, shaking his head, rocking from side to side. "This isn't going to work."

"What isn't going to work?" I was appalled, and beginning to feel acutely anxious.

"*We* aren't going to work," he said, sobbing some more.

Like the use of reverse psychology on a child, his words sent me into a defensive posture. I immediately contradicted him, trying to calm him down.

"Why would you say that? There's no reason to believe we aren't going to 'work,' just because I want to see the show we bought tickets to see."

I tried frantically to reassure him that this wasn't about our relationship. He stopped crying, but he still wouldn't get up from the bed. I gave up and stayed in with him for the rest of the evening. I reluctantly, resentfully, had sex with him, even though I was fuming.

At six-thirty the next morning we went for a walk along the beach, in a heavy, sunless silence. It was windy, cool and cloudy, shades of white and grey. I felt miserable and manipulated. I dreaded the embarrassment of running into people we knew at breakfast.

I was also haunted by the meaning behind Charlie's sudden melodramatic tears. I knew his behaviour wasn't normal, but I was afraid that if I tried to raise it with him, he would become upset again.

Gradually, I came to feel that his eccentricities were the price I had to pay for the privilege of being with someone so exceptional. I would have to be more open-minded and more sensitive to his fragile feelings.

25

PURGATORY

CHARLIE'S APARTMENT LOOKED LIKE A HIPPY GRAD-
uate student's opium den. There was little natural light. The
air was filled with 1960s jazz and folk music and the faint
smell of old paper, weed and incense. The walls were lined
with shelves of books and hundreds of antique toys and
games and vintage paper memorabilia, from stereoscope
photos of Victorian erotica to souvenirs from the 1939 New
York World's Fair. Charlie regularly, lovingly, pored over his
collections. Much of it was valuable and fragile, and he didn't
want a three-year-old child anywhere near it. I only brought
Ben for a visit once, and had to watch him the whole time.

I downplayed my relationship with Charlie to my family,
and I kept him at more than arm's length from Ben. Since we
lived in different parts of town, it wasn't difficult. I wanted
to spend as much one-on-one time with Ben as I could, and

I didn't want to introduce another male adult into Ben's life. Charlie and I spent most of our time together at his apartment, on days when Ben was with his dad.

Our lifestyles just weren't compatible. While I worked a regular nine-to-five day, Charlie only worked mornings, then smoked marijuana and read encyclopedias and reference books while lying on the couch or in the bath all through the afternoon, researching the next morning's stories. He ate a frightening amount of fast food, and drank a bottle of red wine every evening. I rarely kept alcohol in the house, didn't smoke and was uncomfortable with what struck me as his decadence.

Charlie had his own unique and thoroughly considered view on every subject, and he could be fascinating and provocative. I sometimes found his opinions discomfiting, and we had lively philosophical and political debates and sometimes heated arguments. The more topics we discussed, the more naive, narrow-minded and inexperienced I felt compared to him. When Charlie defended himself for having had numerous affairs with married women during his university days, he made me feel provincial and Puritan. He maintained a very close relationship with his estranged partner, which I found threatening, and he told me I was being immature. He was critical of my conventional notions of feminism and fascinated by the subject of female power. He often opined that his stay-at-home mother had enjoyed an enviable life, pampered and cosseted, while his father spent his life trapped in a job that was unglamorous and unfulfilling. Growing up, he had found his mother fascinating, and his father merely sad.

"Women are the lucky sex," he liked to say. "Men feel enormous pressure to financially support them, to physically defend them, to flatter them. And then women hold all the power in sexual relationships. They get to decide yes or no, now or later." He thought women had nothing to complain about. Given my own experience of Catholic patriarchy, I had to disagree.

From the start of our relationship, Charlie set out to introduce me to his favourite things. He was determined to fill in the considerable gaps in my cultural knowledge and he relished the role of mentor. I needed to catch up on a whole generation of "cool." He introduced me to TV shows like *The Prisoner* and *Twin Peaks*, and to the music of Miles Davis and Bob Dylan.

But his most ambitious tutoring was in the field of erotica. First, he brought me into a porn shop that he seemed very familiar with, and I tried desperately to hide my natural embarrassment. He produced reading assignments, like the Erotic Adventures of Sleeping Beauty series and *Candy*. Next were pornographic films. He rented VHS copies of seventies classics like *Deep Throat* and *Behind the Green Door*. He watched me watch them, like a professor of anthropology doing research. I was determined to keep an open mind. It was high time that I shook hands with the real world.

Eventually, he brought home sex props and toys, beginning

with handcuffs, and would produce them from his closet with some trepidation, cautiously reading my face, hopeful and apprehensive. What would I tolerate? What would offend me?

I did have limits I wasn't willing to push. The dog collar and leash went back into the closet and stayed there. I decided I was not cut out to be a dominatrix. He often suggested a threesome but I wasn't game, and I had to remind him of that several times. He bought a Polaroid camera and took dozens of erotic photos of me. I made a concerted effort to play along. Hadn't I done that all my life?

My psychiatrist noticed that my mood was getting darker and became concerned. He suggested we increase the frequency of my appointments to twice a week. And after having been off them for a year or so, I started back on antidepressants.

Charlie and I saw each other several times a week for about two years. However conflicted I felt during that time, I came around to his way of thinking about us. We had a unique and intense psychological bond, even if it was based on mutual mental distress. Twice, when I came close to breaking up with him, he was able to convince me that the problem lay not with our relationship but with my own personal demons. The worse I felt, the more convincing I found him.

One day, as Charlie ran his hands over some lingerie he'd bought for me, I realized he was trembling with a nervousness or ecstasy that he wanted me to witness. In the space of a minute, I suddenly realized his attraction to the lingerie wasn't only about how it looked on me. It was about how it felt against his skin. It was about how it might look on him. I was surprised, but determined to roll with it.

Eventually, we were buying lingerie just for him, size large. Over the next year, I helped him build a substantial wardrobe of women's clothing. At first, he only dressed up for sex with me, but later, he dressed up when he was alone. He said it gave him profound psychological comfort, and of this I had no doubt. I witnessed a calm euphoria wash over him when he was wearing women's clothes. It was genuine and to his core.

I was intrigued by Charlie's new cross-dressing identity, and suspected it wasn't entirely new to him, but that he'd never felt the freedom to explore it before. I was evolving into a sex therapist, helping Charlie to deal with something that was psychologically profound. It gave me a certain sense of purpose. I became convinced that the Catholic Church's great failure was its dogged adherence to the simplistic view that sexuality should serve procreation alone, a belief that only seemed perverse to me now, the naive and malign cause of centuries of woe, for women and men alike. Human sexuality was surely vastly more complex and powerful than any conservative religion was willing to admit or allow its laypeople.

The trouble with Charlie's fantasies and fetishes was that I didn't happen to share most of them. I felt increasingly disconnected from him, as though I was merely providing him with a service, doing him a favour. I was participating in sex with little joy or desire.

The following spring, I was notified that the house I was renting in the Beaches had been repossessed by my landlady's creditors. Ben and I had to find a new home quickly. I was in a panic. We had enjoyed living there for two and a half years, a record for me, and I hated to have to move. My savings had slowly diminished since the separation from Gordon, but I made an offer on a small duplex in Riverdale, hoping I could rent out the upper unit to help pay the mortgage. I didn't qualify for the financing, and the offer fell through.

Charlie then surprised me, stepping in and saying that he would be willing to help me out by going together with me on a house purchase. I was reluctant at first, but then agreed on the condition that we would buy a duplex as co-owners and live in separate units. He would provide most of the down payment, and I would cover most of the mortgage payments, since I was working full-time and he wasn't. With a duplex, I reasoned that if we broke up, we could live separate lives and stay out of each other's way.

A real estate agent showed us several duplexes in Riverdale, but Charlie was unimpressed by all of them. I assured him that he could claim whichever was the nicer unit, but he still wasn't happy. Then, at Charlie's request, she showed us a single-family home. It was a modern, open-concept renovation in monochromatic shades of grey with steel accents, a look completely foreign to my traditionalist taste. Charlie fell in love with the oversized, fully mirrored bathroom with a large Jacuzzi tub. There was a third-floor loft. It was the only house we saw that he liked.

Time was running out on my lease. Charlie was the one with the most cash, so I caved in. We agreed to buy the house. He would take the big room on the third floor, and Ben and I would have the two second-floor bedrooms.

—

While I continued to see my parents weekly, my mother had met Charlie only a few times, and I was nervous about breaking the news to her that he and I were going to buy a house together. For one thing, no one in my family had ever lived "in sin" before. When I got up the nerve to tell her, she said little but looked worried. Then, a few days later, she phoned me with a sense of urgency, saying she'd had a very upsetting dream. She'd dreamed that she was frantically trying to stop me from moving in with Charlie because she knew I was secretly in love with someone else. I was about to make a terrible mistake. She said she woke up with a jolt, deeply distressed and sobbing. Even now, on the phone, she sounded very emotional.

I didn't know what to say. This was the last thing I'd expected to hear. There was another man at work I was somewhat attracted to, but there was no way my mother would have known this. I had only mentioned him to her once in passing.

"Ben and I need to find a new place to live fast," I said. "It's a lovely house in Riverdale, right near a big park. I think everything will be fine. We're going to keep separate bedrooms," I added, though I could tell this didn't reassure her.

"I think you should reconsider, Gail."

Her voice didn't contain a hint of the moral objection I might have expected, only a kind of dread. I told her not to worry. We were going to be tenants-in-common, not joint tenants like a married couple. It would be practical and affordable.

⤴

Charlie and I moved in together. His collection of memorabilia, antique toys, games and trinkets was so vast that it filled the entire third floor. There was no way he would part with any of it, and there was no space left for a bed. We would have to share the front bedroom on the second floor after all. I felt manipulated but I resigned myself to it, in order to keep the peace.

Very soon after the move, I began to feel as though Ben and I were living in Charlie's house. Because he was working only part-time, he spent much more time at home than I did. He settled in first, and his books and music and belongings dominated the space. His lifestyle was soon getting on my nerves, from his tobacco and marijuana smoking to his diet to his pattern of lying around all day on the couch in threadbare T-shirts and track pants. He never sat upright if he could avoid it. He spent long stretches of time locked in the bath, then left choking clouds of talcum powder in the air. He was constantly filing his nails, or picking out one of the six tunes he could play on his guitar. When he wasn't playing his guitar, he played CDs of the same narrow range of his favourite vintage folk and jazz music over and over again throughout the day.

With every passing month, there were more things about him that grated on me. I felt that he was exhaling his troubled spirit into every corner of the house and there was no oxygen left for me and Ben.

A few months after we'd moved in together, his widowed mother flew into town from Winnipeg for a gathering of extended family at the home of cousins in the north end of Toronto. As usual, Charlie was uncomfortable during the entire visit, although these were his closest relatives. I was struck by how emotionally distant he was from all of them, how little effort he made to engage them, even his mother.

At one point during the preparations for dinner, he wanted the two of us to go for a walk while he had a smoke. I felt I should be helping out in the kitchen, and the timing seemed rude, but he insisted. I walked with him along the sidewalk of the North Toronto neighbourhood under a cloud of disillusionment. For all the intense emotion in our relationship, the interdependence, the clinging and clawing, tension and turmoil—all things I'd taken to be aspects of our love—I began to see him in a new and depressing light.

I reluctantly realized I didn't like raising my son in this disturbed atmosphere. Suddenly, at five years old, Ben had started waking up every hour or two of the night and knocking on our bedroom door. Each time, Charlie would tense up, and I could tell that Ben was getting on his nerves. Charlie, now in his midforties, had never lived with a child before—and had never wanted to.

More importantly, I feared that Charlie was getting on my son's nerves too, and that this was why he was reaching out to me through the night. I began spending half of every night in Ben's bedroom, cuddling him until he slipped back to sleep, and then dozing off beside him in his bed. I would wake up after an hour and return to my bed, only to have Ben show up at the door again an hour later to repeat the routine. I was surviving on catnaps like a nursing mother, waking up exhausted each morning and dragging Ben off to kindergarten before I went to work. Meanwhile, Charlie languished around the house smoking and listening to Miles Davis.

Within three months of moving in together, I knew I'd made a terrible mistake that would be costly in every way. The weight of the realization was crushing. I couldn't believe I'd been so stupid. As I began to show signs of my irritation, our relationship began to unravel, and Charlie's already high anxiety bubbled over. He bit his nails until they bled. He had sudden and dramatic crying spells. He played Bob Dylan's "Sad-Eyed Lady of the Lowlands" on a loop, over and over and over again, its lyrics about a "saintlike face" and a "ghostlike soul" echoing all through the house while he stretched out stoned and bleary-eyed on the couch. He was the saddest man in the world, and he wanted me to remember that I was the saddest woman. We were meant for each other, and no one else would ever be good enough and sad enough for either of us.

It took almost a year to negotiate our separation. We got caught up in an excruciating marathon of philosophical and psychological debates over the nature of our relationship—debates that echoed his original courtship speech, only now with more tears and moral recriminations. He argued that I was simply hell-bent on self-destruction, since it was so clearly in my best interest to stay with him. Only he could understand me. Only he could keep me together.

He knew how to strike a nerve. Hadn't I always been misunderstood before him? Hadn't I always been unbalanced before him? Besides, how bad would it look if we broke up so soon after moving in together? What would my mother think? And how disruptive would it be for my son? Charlie had begun to see a therapist himself.

"She wants to know why I care more about Ben's welfare than you do," he said.

I fought back with the reasons why I felt we weren't compatible, why the relationship wasn't working—it was as if I couldn't walk away from him without winning the argument, without seeing him concede defeat. Without his blessing. But he held fast to his own convictions. He was the stronger debater, and he always got in the last word.

I began to question myself to my core. Was it possible that I still loved him, and was in a masochistic state of self-denial? Or had I never really loved him at all? Had my instincts ever been right about anything in my entire life? What was wrong with me? Was I simply seriously mentally ill after all?

I began to imagine that if I didn't break up with him, perhaps I could outlive him. He was eight years older; he smoked and drank heavily, got no exercise and had a bad diet. I fantasized about him dying prematurely of natural causes. How many more years might he have? How many more years of Ben's life would I be willing to tolerate him? One night in bed, my despair at feeling trapped with Charlie was so great that I slipped into a moment of complete hysteria. I was crying so hard that I had never felt such a loss of emotional control before, and it was terrifying.

Charlie began writing on a detective novel while I was at work. The crime case involved a man who murdered his neighbour when the neighbour inadvertently discovered his secret transvestism. I read it and found it more than a little bit chilling. He was very pleased with the manuscript and hoped to get it published. He was hurt when he couldn't get help from former CBC colleagues with publishing contacts.

Charlie had always struck me as a deep well of secrets, but now he began to make a series of more intimate confessions. He told me he'd had a porn magazine habit for many years that he'd kept completely hidden from me. He regularly bought magazines from the tiny convenience store around the corner from our house. He looked amused as he told me the normally cheery Korean lady behind the counter always seemed so sad when she rang them up for him. He said he indulged in daily, elaborate masturbation rituals involving cut-out pictures of naked women. There were other sexual secrets from his past that he now disclosed, and that I found more disturbing. Finally, he divulged that he'd had a psychiatric assessment as a teenager and had received a diagnosis of schizoid personality disorder.

These revelations weren't confessions in the Catholic sense. He wasn't looking for forgiveness, from me or anyone else. He insisted that he regretted nothing about his life, and had nothing to apologize for, and I believed him. I, on the other hand, regretted everything. That was my weakness, he said. Perhaps his disclosures were an effort to deepen our bond, but they didn't have that effect.

I began to suspect that Charlie's biggest fear was to lose me as a sex partner. I simply knew too much for him to let me walk away. In the end, we only reached an agreement to separate when I promised him that I was prepared to remain "friends," hinting that I would even be open to maintaining sexual relations. I knew I was giving him false hope, but it worked. He agreed to start sleeping on the third-floor couch, and to put the house up for sale. During the lull in the storm, I found a new apartment and began packing.

Our false diplomacy broke down in the week before I moved out. While he was away from the house one day, I found the hidden stash of Polaroid pictures he'd taken of me over the last several years. Some I had been comfortable with at the time he took them, but some I had not. Now, I watched a couple hundred semi-nude erotic photos of me blacken, bubble and burn in acrid smoke on our charcoal barbeque. My heart was pounding. I knew Charlie would be livid when he discovered what I'd done, and I was afraid. But I was also relieved beyond measure. I was refusing to be a part of his vast collection (and I did not trust that he wouldn't have used the photos against me).

I wasn't home when he returned to discover what I'd done. He left a screaming, raging message on my phone accusing me of ruthlessness and rape, violation and theft. I kept the recording and later played it for my lawyer so that she understood my situation. He then rifled through the bedroom until he found my journal, which was filled with my private fantasies of escaping from him. He left blood smears on the pages.

I was too ashamed to ask work friends who knew both Charlie and me for support during the breakup. When Ben and I finally moved out of that house, it was with the help of some of my old York University grad school friends. Although we had slowly drifted apart over the years, they mobilized themselves when I reached out, showing up on my moving day like angels of mercy when I didn't know where else to turn.

That evening, surrounded by boxes in our tiny new apartment north of Danforth Avenue, I sat reading to Ben on a mattress on the floor and felt that this was the happiest day of my entire life. I was thirty-seven years old, and whether or not I deserved it, I had been given another chance. I had escaped from the closest thing to hell I'd ever known.

⤙

Several years after our breakup, when my car was stopped at a red light on St. Clair Avenue, Charlie crossed directly in front of my bumper to board a streetcar. If he had turned his head left, he would have seen me, nothing between us but the front hood of my car. But he didn't. He walked over to the streetcar and disappeared inside. There was more grey hair than I remembered on his head and in his beard, but otherwise he looked unchanged. For all the melodrama of our dissolution, his life had gone on fine without me.

The intensity of my reaction to seeing him again shocked me. It took nearly half an hour for my heart to stop pounding, my throat to relax. Why, after all these years, did Charlie still strike such fear in me, as though he possessed an unearthly power that could have dragged me back into his dark orbit again? I was more afraid of him than anyone I'd ever known. Like he had the codes to all my nightmares.

A dozen years later, I heard from an old CBC friend that Charlie had died. I was overcome with emotion. Sadness, regret and relief. I heard about a memorial service planned by radio colleagues and friends, and I knew there would be heartfelt praise for him. I thought briefly that I should attend, but I couldn't bear the thought. I no longer hated him, but the year that I'd lived with him had been the worst of my life. His death meant that my fear of accidentally running into him again was finally over. For that I was truly grateful.

⊀

One of the acts I would always regret was giving Charlie the scapular that had been a gift from Matthew in high school. I had kept the scapular, with its promise to protect the wearer from the eternal fires of hell, in a safe place for years, but one day I'd shown it to Charlie, and he was completely charmed. He had to have it for his collection. I wish I'd had the courage to ask for it back before I moved out, but I didn't.

I wonder if it worked for him. I hope so. Nobody deserves eternal fire.

26

BENEDICTION

IN THE SPRING OF 1993, IN THE FINAL MONTHS OF my life with Charlie, I took my mother on a day trip to a farm where Catholic pilgrims had claimed to experience the presence of the Blessed Virgin Mary. I was working on a documentary for *Man Alive* on the subject we casually referred to as "apparitions of the BVM" and had already visited the farm for a film shoot a few weeks before.

It was an ordinary Ontario farmhouse just outside the tiny town of Marmora, with several acres of open field out back and a ring of forest beyond. Spread out among the trees that marked the boundary of the field were homemade signs, each representing one of the fourteen stations of the cross— a pictorial narrative of Jesus's crucifixion designed to empha-size the brutality of his death.

The property was open to the public, and there were

busloads of groups from Toronto's more evangelical Catholic churches. I hadn't heard of this farm before I started research-ing the topic of Marian apparitions in Canada, but it was popular among that fringe of the Catholic faithful most inter-ested in visions and miracles.

My relationship with my mother had become strained over my troubles with Charlie. She was unsurprised that our cohabitation was coming to a wretched end, and she was also unsympathetic. I was lying in the bed I'd made. She was disil-lusioned with me and that bothered me, but I was determined to try to cheer her up, to win her back. I told her a trip to Marmora would be her Mother's Day present.

On the drive up, I tried hard to engage her in conversation, but she was in a flat mood. After so many years of interest, she now preferred not to know what was going on in my life, and who could blame her? I wondered if she was also suspicious of my motives. She knew I was no longer a practising Catholic. Why take her to this farm where the Blessed Virgin Mary was believed to appear? But perhaps my mother had other things on her mind that day. After all, she had six other adult children, each with their own dreams and dramas, and some-times it was still too easy for me to forget that I wasn't her only child.

The drive up felt long, especially because our conversation was stilted, so it was a relief to finally arrive. We parked in a small lot with a half-dozen other cars and picked up some printed material from the farmhouse porch. We read a brief history of the apparitions and miracles said to have occurred on the property, and the story behind the family's decision to create the stations of the cross in their field out back. I worried that, so far, my mother seemed unimpressed. At least it was nice to be out of the car after the long drive, and we had a perfectly pleasant country stroll ahead of us. It was a warm afternoon in May, and we both wore sun hats.

Each station of the cross was marked by a simple image and title on a wooden plaque: *Jesus is condemned to death. Jesus carries his cross. Jesus falls a first time*. At the foot of each station were religious icons, pictures of loved ones, plastic flowers, all left behind by pilgrims who had walked the stations before us, praying and making supplications. A few dozen other visitors were making their way across the property that day, walking slowly from station to station, often kneeling and mumbling prayers, but it wasn't crowded. We were able to keep a respectable distance from them.

My mother and I spoke little to each other, pausing for an appropriate length of time at each station as if to pray, and then moving on. Perhaps she was really praying, but I suspected she wasn't. She just seemed too tense. I knew *I* wasn't praying.

As we approached the fourth station, titled *Jesus meets his mother*, I immediately smelled a strong scent of roses: the classic sign that Mary is present. I looked down and all around, but could see no roses, or any flowers at all. My next thought was that it was some kind of trick, a special-effects feature planted by the owners. But I couldn't find any source of the fragrance. The air simply smelled of roses, distinctive and unmistakable. I finally turned to my mother.

"Do you smell that?"

"Roses?" she asked, and she gave a solemn nod.

We breathed in deeply, hesitated, and then slowly moved on to the next station. But the mood of the rest of the walk took on a surreal tranquility. We both became much more relaxed. We snapped some photos, and later, when I had them developed, I couldn't resist checking them for any signs of the supernatural: strange lights, shadows, forms. Instead, I only found poorly framed, blurred photos of the two of us, looking expressionless, like we'd both slipped into a trance.

On the long drive home, I felt intense relief. I felt good. I chatted about the latest documentary I was working on, and the director I was working with. I'd mentioned him when describing another story we'd co-produced a year or so before, and she remembered the name Michael. Suddenly, it was as though I'd set off her sixth sense.

"If you wind up with that guy, Gail, I'll have to write you off for good."

At first, this struck me as a complete non sequitur. I was offended. Why was she treating me once again like a wayward teenager with no self-control? And what did she mean by "write me off" anyway? Besides, I could do worse than wind up with Michael. He'd been the first person I'd thought of when she'd told me her upsetting dream the year before, warning me against moving in with Charlie.

After all these years, she could still strike fear in my heart. Which is why, when Michael and I eloped to Las Vegas six months later, we kept it a secret for so long.

⌣

I will never forget the very first time Michael caught my eye. I was coming out of an elevator on the *Man Alive* floor and he was walking down the hall to my right. With his long, swift strides and head held high, he was full of purpose. Just as he flashed by, he looked sideways in my direction and our eyes met. There was a split-second twitch of a smile.

Michael was a freelance TV director working for the CBC at the time, an award-winning veteran of documentary and arts programming in Canada and England. He had a British accent, a Cambridge education and a continental style. He seemed naturally energetic, enthusiastic and optimistic. Not my type at all. He was also tall and dark-haired and handsome, with great bones and large green-brown eyes. He had been working with a colleague of mine on a *Man Alive* show about gospel music, and the next time I saw her, I leaned in and asked, "Why do you always get to work with the cute ones?" She laughed, surprised at me. I had surprised myself as well.

I barely gave him another thought until months later, when my boss asked me to work with Michael on a story about workaholics. During the filming, a psychologist we interviewed pulled me aside and told me that she feared Michael couldn't fully appreciate the dangers of workaholism because he was obviously a workaholic himself. I revealed her misgivings to Michael, not sure how he'd react. He seemed amused. Then he talked about what making documentaries meant to him, and I realized that he wasn't talking about his work as work. He fervently believed in the importance of cultural and political discourse, and the documentary form was his preferred language. I was impressed by his idealism, and his old-world mix of reserve and passion.

A few months later, Michael invited me to join him for a glass of wine after work. I was living with Charlie at that point. Although we knew nothing about each other's personal lives, within twenty minutes of sitting together in a downtown bar, we were exchanging our birth stories. We discovered that death had haunted us both from the day we were born. I told him that my mother believed I was the dead baby she had lost, brought back to life by God. I didn't mention how, for much of my life, I had believed it too. After three years of psychiatric therapy, and my discouraging relationship with Charlie, I no longer cared to dwell too much on questions of miracles or reincarnation.

Michael told me that he was born in London during the Nazi bomb raids in 1941. His mother suffered a brain embolism during his birth and died soon after. His only sibling, a brother five years older, was diagnosed with paranoid schizophrenia while Michael was away at boarding school, and his father died suddenly of a cardiac arrest that same year. We had both survived difficult birth narratives that had affected our families and our whole lives, defining us in dramatic ways.

Later that winter, during a film shoot, we stood side·by side in the vestibule of the Cathedral of Sainte-Anne-de-Beaupré, in a small village north of Quebec City. This was the Catholic church my mother had told me about as a little girl, the most famous in the country for miraculous healings, and we were filming a scene for a *Man Alive* show there. The crutches and leg braces of a hundred healed pilgrims were fixed to huge pillars on either side of the cathedral's central aisle. For me, the setting resonated deeply, if ironically, and I said so. Michael just looked around slowly and said he didn't care much for religion or churches, apart from good organ music and architecture. As for deities, he preferred nature.

During my last months of living with Charlie, when I was at my most distressed and despairing, Michael and I met for coffee and I confided to him about the painful dilemma in my personal life, unable to decide whether to leave the relationship or stay. He seemed completely perplexed by why I would stay in a relationship that obviously made me so unhappy.

I tried to explain to him that while Charlie was a difficult person in many ways, he had a brilliant and unique mind. Later, Michael would say that I had sounded to him like someone who'd been brainwashed by a cult leader. When I confessed that I'd struggled my whole life with a kind of emotional instability that had led directly to the fix I was now in, he looked at me incredulously and shook his head.

"That's hard to believe," he said. "From the moment I met you, you struck me as a very strong person."

⤙

The first time Michael and I slept together, I thought I was making a conscious decision to have casual sex for the very first time in my life, just for fun. As it turned out, it was fun, but it wasn't casual. From that moment on, I felt a kinship with him that I'd never felt before. I didn't need him to explain it or convince me. He simply said afterwards, "I'm in love with you," and I realized I felt the same way.

Michael was truly a lover of nature, of deep forests and empty beaches, large dogs and long walks. He was also a lover of travel to distant places, from dense tropical cities to rusty old towns, always exploring local music, theatre and dance, going off the beaten path whenever he could. He was unlike anyone I'd met before, a self-reliant spirit who heartily embraced challenges and adventure. He approached everything like a person who felt lucky to be alive. He made me realize that I was lucky too.

Getting married only a few months after we began dating was Michael's idea, and so was the venue. He did all the research and booked the tickets. I would never have dreamed of something so spontaneous and outrageous—spending two nights in the Flamingo Hotel and exchanging vows at The Little Church of the West right on Las Vegas Boulevard. But it felt perfect in every way.

It was a day that had us in tears—first from laughter. We thought we were going to be late for our own wedding, and we ran along the strip all the way from the hotel to the chapel. As they passed us, drivers on the boulevard honked and shouted good-naturedly: "Don't do it!"

Then, as we stood before the minister-for-hire at a tiny altar, he spoke to us with such unexpected poignancy about the meaning of love and commitment that before he was finished, we had tears in our eyes and lumps in our throats, overcome with gratitude for the way his words had touched our hearts.

That afternoon, we cut a clear path through the hotel lobby, past the noisy slot machines and out the huge glass entrance onto the street. We rented a car and drove out of town into the Mojave Desert, where on that warm autumn day, there was a sudden freak snowfall. We left the car at the side of the road and walked into the desert, snowflakes settling in our hair and on our outstretched palms. We joked that the snow was fallout from some military experiment being conducted at a suspicious high-security government installation we'd passed along the highway. Or perhaps it was simply a good omen that, in a town of long odds and last chances, we had found ourselves a sure thing.

We returned to Toronto two days later, and neither of us told a soul. Michael held on to his apartment and we lived separately for another five months. We covered up our marriage for my benefit, because I was loath to break the news to my parents just yet. My mother's comment about writing me off still echoed in my ears, and I thought she should get to know Michael a bit better before I told her he was her new son-in-law.

By Christmas I had broken the news that Michael and I were dating, but I was still reluctant to bring him over to my parents' house to meet the family. I could tell they weren't ready. My mother didn't like that he was divorced and fifteen years older than me.

"How do you know he isn't a playboy?" she asked when I showed her a picture of him. The contrast between Michael and Charlie couldn't have been more striking. But one simple and important difference was the way he treated Ben. Michael was the father of two adult sons and loved children. The first time he slept over, when my bed in my new apartment was still just a mattress on the floor, Ben came to the door in the middle of the night. Michael immediately got up and brought some of Ben's bedding and a pillow back into the room and welcomed my son to set up camp beside us. The next day, Michael suggested that we go shopping for a children's sleeping bag, one decorated with Ben's favourite cartoon characters. He suggested we welcome Ben to join us any night he wanted, so long as he brought along his special sleeping bag and pillow. Ben was very pleased. He knew he was welcome, and as it turned out, that was enough. Within several days, he stopped bothering to come into our room. He was sleeping through the night again, and from that day forward.

⤙

The following spring, Ben and I travelled with Michael to England on our first holiday together. It was Ben's first time on a plane. We rented a car and travelled down to Cornwall and Devon, and up to the ruins of Tintagel Castle, King Arthur's birthplace. We stopped in at Stonehenge, and then stayed in London. We took a boat tour on the Thames, shopped at Hamleys toy store, saw the mummies in the British Museum, hung out in Regent's Park, watched buskers in Covent Garden and admired the stone lions in Trafalgar Square. It was an epic vacation. When we returned, I was brimming with happiness and wanted to share it with my mother. I had the overwhelming urge to tell her the truth. I sat at her kitchen table as I had a thousand times before, and she stood across the room working at the counter. We were alone.

"I'm going to tell you something that I haven't told anyone else, something I've been keeping a secret for six months. Michael and I are married. We eloped to Las Vegas last November."

I don't know what I expected, but not the sharp gasp, the

contorted face. There was a single long sob. With her head hanging low, her voice shaking and barely a whisper, I heard her ask herself, "What's a family for?"

I had never seen her so distraught. She turned her back to me and bent far over the sink. After a longer, sickening silence, I stood up and left the house.

I was devastated, but on my drive home a new sensation took hold of me. It was indignation. You can't spend your whole life trying to make your mother happy, asking for permission to do things she can't understand. Asking for her blessing to live your life. After all, hadn't she broken her own father's heart by marrying my dad without his blessing? And by moving a thousand miles away from her home? I didn't feel a second of regret for having married Michael. It was the best decision I'd ever made. Someday, she would come to understand this, but I would soon be thirty-eight years old. I couldn't put my life on hold until she was ready.

⌇

For a month or so, I stayed away from my parents' house completely. Michael and I were settling into our new home, Ben was finishing his school year and I was busy with *Man Alive*. On Mother's Day, I finally worked up the courage to bring Michael over to meet my family. It had been a full year since my mother and I had visited the farm in Marmora together. She was subdued but polite toward Michael. She even managed to give him a little smile. But she and I didn't make much eye contact, and we only spoke a little. She looked pale and pained.

I didn't know if she'd told anyone else in the family about the elopement. I hadn't. And no one raised it with me. The few times I saw my siblings that summer, I felt an emotional distance from them, even irritation. I assumed there wasn't a lot of goodwill in the family left for me. People aren't always going to understand you, I told myself, and sometimes that's okay. Then, in the late summer, I arrived at my mother's house for a visit and met Glenna in the driveway. She confronted me angrily about when I was going to finally make the news of my marriage public. She was livid that I'd held off for so long.

"Do you know how much you've hurt Mom and Dad?" she asked.

I was surprised by her intensity. I didn't try to defend myself. I felt there would have been disapproval no matter how I'd handled things. But I was stung by her criticism, and worried that I'd caused my parents more pain than I realized.

Michael saw that the rift with my family was weighing on me. Since our first-year anniversary was soon approaching, he suggested that we renew our marriage vows in a traditional church service and invite my family to join us. We could follow the ceremony with a small celebration back at our house. We booked a quaint old Anglican church in the heart of downtown and invited our families and a few close friends to attend. My parents and siblings accepted the invitations without hesitation.

Michael arranged for a colleague who was a professional photographer to take our wedding pictures. But then Glenna surprised me by offering to take our wedding pictures herself with her brand new camera. I explained to Michael that my sister Melanie had taken the pictures at my first wedding, so it was awkward to turn Glenna's offer down now. She was very keen to do it. Michael hesitated, but reluctantly agreed, and cancelled his photographer friend.

This second ceremony was, for us, another joyful experience. Both Ben and Michael's adult son Justin were in high spirits. (His younger son, Zeno, was attending university in England.) My parents were reserved, but they were there and making an effort. My brothers and sisters, their husbands and wives and children, all seemed in genial moods. They all bore wedding presents. Glenna snapped her camera throughout the ceremony.

Back at our house, as I was putting out the food and serving drinks, I heard a deep gasp from the living room, followed by screams and squeals and a swell of horrified amusement. Glenna had just come across the bag of new film I'd bought her, still unopened in her purse, and realized she'd taken all of our wedding pictures with an empty camera.

We were left without a single photograph of the ceremony: no happy couple, no pictures of my son or family members. Glenna was mortified and speechless. I suspected my siblings appreciated the delicious irony of this catastrophe. It was as if, on that day, my punishment had been meted out—for soaking up more than my share of familial attention since the day I was born.

⊹

As it turned out, it wasn't long before my parents genuinely warmed to Michael. My mother developed a sincere appreciation for him, always asking after him each time we spoke on the phone—about his film projects, his health, his sons. And Michael had a special fondness for my father, and sought out a place beside him at every family gathering. When we visited, I began to feel a kind of peace and acceptance in my mother's presence that I hadn't experienced since I'd lived with her during my pregnancy. I felt I had finally, without reserve, won her blessing.

⊹

One question had continued to gnaw at me after so many years. Whatever had happened to my old friend Matthew? Whether out of curiosity, guilt or a need for closure, I wanted to know. Occasionally, I searched his name on the internet, but could never find a trace of him. Finally, I tracked down an old high school friend of his, who told me that he'd heard Matthew was living in a monastery in Vermont. He thought it was a Benedictine priory. I researched Benedictine monasteries in Vermont and wrote to them, but they knew no one by his name. I wrote to his old alma mater, Magdalen College, but they had no record of him after graduation. Finally, I searched online for Carthusian monasteries. There was only one in all of North America, also in Vermont. There were fifteen monks living there as hermits, in total silence and seclusion in their separate little cells. They were completely cut off from the outside world, without electricity or possessions of any kind, living a medieval monastic life. They each tended a little garden for their only source of food. Hand-chopped firewood was their only fuel. When they died, they were buried in unmarked graves. Could Matthew be one of them?

Eventually, I succeeded in tracking down Matthew's brother, Mark, who had attended the same high school, on LinkedIn. I sent him a message that included my phone number and he called me. He confirmed that Matthew had entered the Carthusian monastery in 1985. He was still there. Mark assured me that he believed Matthew had found happiness in his life, but he had a confession to make.

"In high school, I always hoped you two would wind up together. You had a rare and special relationship. You could have been my sister-in-law."

I thanked him, and hung up the phone before he could hear me start to cry. I had broken my own heart over Matthew such a long time ago. Now my tears were for him.

27

EPIPHANY

MY MOTHER PHONED ME TO TELL ME ABOUT A nightmare my father had had the night before. In his dream, I had been murdered in a ritual sacrifice at the hands of some religious cult. When my dad recovered my dead body, he cut off my head, then wrapped it in a blanket and brought it to my mother. He carefully placed the bundle in her arms, and when she opened the blanket and looked at my face, I opened my eyes. That's when my father woke up with a jolt.

"He was completely traumatized," she said.

My mother and I both agreed it was a pretty interesting dream, but neither of us ventured an interpretation. I didn't feel ready for an open discussion with my parents about me and the other Gail. I wondered if I ever would.

A few months later, my mother surprised me with a confession of her own. It was a quiet Sunday afternoon, and I sat alone with her on her porch. She seemed nervous, and spoke cautiously.

"Years ago," she said, "I thought about your birth, and how I hadn't had any labour pain, and I began to ask myself if it was possible that I had misremembered the details all along."

I felt mildly alarmed. Where was she going with this?

"I know now I was suffering from a kind of mental illness after the car accident and right through my thirties," she said, a reference to what she'd started to tell me some years before. "I began to wonder if perhaps I was so unhinged at that time of your birth that I had somehow blocked the labour pain out of my memory."

She went on to say that this question haunted her, and there was only one way to put her mind at rest. She needed to talk to someone who had actually been present during my birth. So she looked up the name of the physician who'd been on call at the hospital that night in 1956, and managed to track him down by phone. He was retired. She explained to him that, many years ago, he had delivered her baby. She described the birth, and how she had no memory of having any labour pain. She wanted to know if he remembered her. Did he remember that birth?

"Yes," he said, without hesitation. "I do remember you, and I do remember that birth, after all these years. And no, you did not appear to experience any labour pain at all."

It was something that had stayed with him, he said, because when they spoke afterwards, she had told him about losing a baby girl the year before, and how I looked identical to that baby she had lost.

I wondered why my mother was telling me this now, many years after she'd contacted the doctor. Perhaps she thought I could finally handle knowing that she had once questioned her own memory of my birth. And now, she seemed to want to set the record straight, once and for all. It was as if she was saying, *I never lied to you about your birth. I told you the truth.*

In a sense, we were back where we started, she and I. She was standing by the story she told me when I was four: she had no labour pain during my birth, and I looked just like the other Gail. Those were the facts. Whether or not that meant I was the rebirth of the other Gail remained unspoken. Who could ever say such a thing with certainty? We can only know what we believe. In my heart, I no longer believed it. But I still believed that perhaps she believed it. And through all these years, hadn't that always been what mattered most to me? What she believed? Because religious conviction had never really been the crux of the matter. It had always been my belief in my mother.

⤵

While I felt myself getting closer to my mother, her health was failing. She had lived with chronic pain for as long as I could remember, between her osteoporosis and mild scoliosis, and frequent backaches and headaches. For years, she had suffered from digestive problems too, but they seemed to be getting worse. She had always been active, but I was struck now by how slowly she moved. She was only sixty-five, and yet she seemed to wince with every step.

Her family doctor was convinced that her abdominal problems were gynecological, and put her on hormone replacement therapy for several months. When that didn't work, my mother was told she needed a hysterectomy.

Jeannie stayed at the hospital during my mother's surgery, and I headed over to join her after work. I found Jeannie alone in the hospital hallway, standing up against the wall, frozen. When she saw me, she broke down in tears. The surgeon had found cancer. It was at an advanced stage, metastasized throughout my mother's abdomen. It was inoperable.

My mother was angry about the earlier misdiagnoses, and she questioned whether the hormone replacement therapy had made the cancer spread faster. But her anger soon turned to stoicism, and a determination to go through a course of chemotherapy with a positive mind. And she did. I regularly met her and my father in the waiting area of Sunnybrook Hospital's oncology clinic, sat with them until my mother was taken away for a session, and then stayed with my father until she came back out. I had a flexible and forgiving workplace, and I wanted to be there for my parents. I focused on gathering as much medical information as possible, spinning it in the most positive light I could for everyone's sake.

Shortly after beginning her chemo treatments, my mother set herself up at a heavy old electric typewriter in one of the downstairs bedrooms and began to write a memoir. She said she wanted to record some of her early memories while she was still able. For many weeks, while undergoing chemo, she tapped away at the keys. I had never known her to write before, and her focus was impressive. Once or twice I stood at the bedroom doorway as she typed, but I never ventured inside. Then one day, she suddenly stopped writing, and the manuscript disappeared. I never asked if I could read it. I didn't want to. The idea made me nervous, though I didn't ask myself why.

After about six months of chemo, my mother's condition seemed to stabilize. We allowed ourselves to believe that her cancer had gone into remission. But only a few months later, her prognosis became even more dire. After a temporary slowdown in growth, the tumours were making up for lost time and growing even more rapidly. The doctor told my mother she would die within months.

After the doctor left, my mother and I stood in the examining room and leaned on each other, pressing forehead to forehead in silence. I felt her heavy sadness, her resignation, her acceptance, and her incredible strength. This news brought about a sea change. For the first time, she told me she loved me. For the first time, I told her I loved her. For the first time, we hugged and held each other.

All throughout that last summer, my mother faced her

death with quiet acceptance. She said she wasn't afraid. She was only worried about leaving my father behind, and whether the family would take care of him after she was gone. He had always been on the periphery while everyone vied for her attention. She worried that he would be forgotten. I tried to reassure her that we would never neglect our father, that we would take care of him, and that everyone was going to be fine.

My parents' house became a meeting place for my siblings and me, and we each pitched in. One day in July, I arrived at the house to find my mother waiting for me on the porch. She asked if I'd join her for a stroll. Walking even a half block was a struggle for her, and this was the last time I saw her try. As we moved slowly, arm in arm, she began talking about her father, about his terrible temper, and how he used it to control his wife and children. Then she told me a story. During the Depression, food was scarce. Her mother struggled to feed her family of ten from her small garden. She had just set the table for dinner, the food carefully portioned out. She called everyone to eat, but her husband—my mother's father—arrived home in a terrible mood. He was livid with two of their sons, whom he suspected of stealing. He was a towering man, six foot four, and could be terrifying when in a rage. He confronted the boys, and when they pleaded innocent, he grabbed the table with both hands and flipped it upside down, sending all the plates of food flying.

What my mother remembered most after her mother's scream and the crash was the petrifying silence. Her mother then got down on her hands and knees, a heart-sickened look on her face, and tried to salvage bits of food among the shards. At the time, she was angry at her mother for failing to stand up to her father. But she knew her mother hadn't dared. That was how much control he wielded in the family.

I had never heard this story before.

"My father loved us," she continued, "but he struggled to control the family with his anger. In every way he could. That was why he sent me away to a convent school. Because as I was entering puberty, he was afraid that he was going to lose control of me. He knew the convent would control me."

This was the first time I'd heard her speak of going to the convent school as anything but a privilege and a salvation. By now, we had walked a block or so and we needed to turn around. I worried that we'd gone too far from the house, but I was also captivated by what my mother was saying.

"All my life, I've tried to control my children in just the same way that my father, and then the nuns, controlled me. It did a lot of damage, and I regret it. I thought I was doing it for my children's sake, trying to protect them. But I know now that when you try to control your children, and when you are always fearful of losing your children, it only backfires. It only makes everything worse."

She spoke with a powerful sense of reflection and sorrow, and I knew she was thinking of all her children. Her love had sometimes seemed conditional. That day, I thought she was trying to assure me that she had always loved us, every single one of us, all along and completely. I was deeply moved, and I wanted her to keep talking. But she had fallen quiet, overcome with fatigue. We slowly headed back toward the house in silence.

Over the final few months, there were the inevitable, painful transitions. The master bedroom became my mother's hospital room. She reached the point where she could no longer eat solid food of any kind, and then the point where she could barely drink her beverage meal replacements either. She had difficulty getting in and out of bed to use the bathroom on her own. She needed to be on an IV drip. She needed a catheter. She needed a morphine pump. Nonetheless, her mood was surprisingly light. She often seemed happy, grateful, even blessed.

I recall us laughing one day as I awkwardly helped her from her bed to the bathroom—she was attached to the IV pole and I tried to support her, holding her up under her armpits, unsure whether she could still stand on her own. She was as light as a child. Later in the afternoon, she made fun of me in front of my sisters, insisting on demonstrating how I had tried to help her walk. She actually struggled to her feet and stood behind me, pushing me up from the armpits, my arms above my head, laughing at how I had forced her to walk. Soon after, when I announced that I had to get back home, she held out her hands to my face and kissed me goodbye. She smiled sadly at me.

"I'm sorry for giving you a hard time."

Her words went straight to my heart. I floated out of her house that day, my eyes streaming with tears of gratitude. *She said she had given me a hard time. She said she was sorry.*

She wanted to die at home. Jeannie courageously learned how to operate the homecare medical machinery and assumed primary responsibility for my mother's support. Toward the end, we took turns staying at her side through the night. The first time I tried to sleep beside my mother on her bed, I stayed awake listening to the hum of her machinery—the IV drip, the pump administering morphine at intervals, the barely audible serenity tapes of ocean waves she played on a little cassette recorder. It was a long night filled with gentle sounds. She fumbled with a prayer card, an image of Mother Mary, leaning it just so against her cassette recorder to cover the little "on" light that was bothering her eyes. She reached her fingers out to my pyjama top, a silvery-taupe paisley silk, a present from Michael.

"Beautiful," she said. "Is that pillow uncomfortable? Are you managing to get any sleep at all?"

Later, as we realized that our presence by her side was keeping my mother awake, my sisters and I would take turns sleeping on an air mattress on the floor at the foot of her bed.

During those last days, we sat on my mother's bed, held her hands, gave her extra doses of morphine. My father shuffled from room to room, mute, bleary-eyed, in pain. One afternoon, she drifted in and out of sleep as several of us sat with her. She was heavily drugged and only barely aware of who we were. At one point, she opened her eyes and looked directly at me. Her face lit up with a smile. "My beautiful daughter!" she said. As much as I might have wished it, I knew it wasn't me she saw. It was the other Gail, claiming her rightful place among us at our mother's deathbed.

In my forty-two years, I had never had an open conversation about my relationship to the other Gail with anyone in my family. No one had ever raised the subject with me. Now, it was as if she had suddenly, finally, broken to the surface of our family. As Linda, my father and I were sitting in the living room while my mother slept upstairs, Linda put a question to my father. Without warning, without context, with a tone of slight agitation, as though the question had finally forced itself upon her after years of silent wondering: "What was going through your mind when Mom thought that Gail was the other Gail?"

I was thrown back by the shock of it. I had never had the courage to imagine, let alone ask, this question.

My father hesitated for only a moment, and then he said, "I guess I believed it too."

I felt an overwhelming rush of anger. *No wonder. No wonder I believed it too. Who was I, a tiny child, to play the only skeptic in the house? Who was I to question their miracle?*

I had always blamed myself for being too gullible, too naive, too easily flattered by my mother's story. But my father had believed it too. As intense as my anger was, it passed like a freak summer storm. I was left with a painful image for the first time: my father's grief after the other Gail's death. He lost his baby daughter too. Who doesn't long for a miracle?

My mother died on September 18, 1998, while I was driving along the highway toward her house. I stepped inside the front door shortly after to find my family gathering to meet me in the hallway.

"Mom died," Linda said. A loud cry. Glenna threw her arms around me.

Linda and Jeannie had been with her at the end. Later, Linda told us about a discussion she'd had with the palliative care doctor who'd been attending to our mother, visiting the house during the last few weeks. He said he had been very moved by her character. "She faced death with great dignity," he had told Linda.

"But it was so sad, so tragic," he had added, "that she'd been haunted all her life by the death of her baby girl."

I felt that I might faint. *Haunted all her life by the death of her baby girl?* Why would she have told this doctor, whom she barely knew, that she had been "haunted all her life"? Hadn't she believed her baby girl had come back from the dead? Hadn't she believed her dead baby girl was *me*?

Later that day, I stood in the family room, staring at the picture of the other Gail on my dad's lap, the same picture that had found its way into the bottom of my dresser drawer decades before. After my siblings and I moved out, my mother hung it on the wall next to her children's graduation pictures and family portraits. Between *Gail* and *Gallant* in the photo's inscription, I noticed for the very first time a small arrow in a different colour of ink. I had to take the picture down from the wall and out of its frame to see what the arrow was pointing to. Written above was the name *Marie*. Though she'd used a different-coloured pen, it was unmistakably my mother's hand.

I stood in the family room holding the picture and felt like a single person for the first time in my life, as if I'd survived a surgical procedure to separate conjoined twins. I was just the fourth-born of Lawrence and Maria Gallant's eight children. Like a cauterized wound, it was a searing, healing pain.

Linda wrote my mother's death notice for the newspaper. I saw it only after it was published. It named my mother's children, ending with a sixth daughter with the hyphenated name Gail-Marie. The other Gail had been renamed. She had a name of her own. And now I did too.

In the few days that followed my mother's death, I had one pressing, pounding question. I finally found the courage to ask Jeannie.

"When do you think Mom stopped believing that I was the other Gail?"

Despite all the years in which we'd talked so freely, I had never discussed the other Gail with her before. I was nervous about raising it now. But she didn't seem surprised. She thought about it before she answered.

"In a way," she said, "I don't think she ever believed it." She paused and then she added, "And in another way, she probably never stopped."

On the day of my mother's funeral, my brother John told us about the dream he'd had the night before. In it, he walked into a white room and there was our mother, holding a baby. She reassured him that all was well. He said she was smiling, looking down at the baby cradled in her arms.

✧

Fifteen years after my mother's death, my father was still living a full life. He had long since stopped binge drinking and smoking cigarettes—his one indulgence now was chocolate-dipped marshmallow cookies. Even though he'd lost half of his tongue to oral cancer years before, had since endured years of treatment for bladder cancer, and had recently lost his left leg to peripheral vascular disease, he was lively and independent. His first heavily sedated words after the amputation surgery were "Piece of cake!" I took him to countless doctors' appointments, and he always emerged from painful medical procedures with a big grin and two thumbs up. He would joke that the only reason he wasn't dead yet was because my mother, already up in heaven, was in no great hurry to see him.

In his later years, he loved to entertain us with stories, making sure each one of his children heard about his latest misadventure. He laughed uncontrollably at a good joke, especially his own. Only now did I believe the rumour I'd heard when I was young, that he could be a different person at work. In his seventies and eighties, after all those early years of emotional distance, he won back the hearts of every one of his children, including me. He was finally engaged, always ready to lend us each a hand in any way he could. And he gave the best advice for car trouble, right to his dying day.

When he was just shy of eighty-eight years old, I sat on the side of his hospital bed on a quiet Sunday afternoon and knew that this time he wasn't going to pull through. I knew he knew it too.

"You've been a wonderful father," I whispered to him.

He jerked his face away from me in a spasm of pain.

"Everybody loves you."

His face relaxed, and he slowly turned back to me. He knew that this time, I was telling him the truth.

For the first time, I broke down in tears in front of him, and he reached out with his frail fingers and slowly stroked the back of my hand, comforting me as he lay dying.

For four days, my brothers and sisters and I kept vigil at his hospital bed. In that flicker of a moment, when I realized my father was dead, the words of a mad woman flew from my mouth, "Dad, don't go!"

His spirit rushed from his body like a bird, off to the left of his bed, in the direction of the window overlooking the hospital parking lot.

28

TESTAMENT

MANY MONTHS AFTER MY MOTHER DIED, I FINALLY found the courage to read the memoir she had written while she was ill. I was afraid that she might not verify my childhood memories of the birth story, the precious details that I'd tucked away and carried around my whole life. But instead, the memoir confirmed my earliest memories, right down to the song the anesthetist sang while he waited for her labour to begin.

It was an untitled first draft, a loose stack of sixty-five pages, all single-spaced lines, with no chapter breaks and no paragraphs. It read like an oral transcript, and my mother's voice was clear and strong. I marvelled at how well she wrote, under such difficult circumstances. She always was a natural storyteller.

Her memoir was filled with colourful characters, lively details and anecdotes about growing up in rural Prince Edward Island in the 1930s and '40s. I'd known so little about my maternal grandmother, who had died when my mother was eight years old, but on these pages, my mother brought her to life. She wrote about the four years she spent in the residential convent school, and the honour of having been chosen valedictorian of her graduating class. She described her first job at the age of sixteen, as a schoolteacher who single-handedly ran a one-room rural schoolhouse for children in grades one to eight. She admitted that she was a strict disciplinarian. And she wrote about her rebellious marriage to my father when she was barely eighteen.

Reading her memoir, it was clear to me that she could have been a writer, should have been a writer. Who knows what she might have achieved if her childhood had been less marked by poverty and tragedy?

Years after she died, I became a writer. I have long stopped caring about God or religion in general, though I still carry a rosary and a few of my mother's holy medals in my purse as mementos, and for good luck. The legacy of my Catholicism is a weakness for the supernatural. I find myself drawn to the idea of ghosts. When Michael and I purchased a derelict farmhouse in Grey County near Georgian Bay for weekend retreats, I became convinced that the old barn at the back of the property was haunted. Eventually I wrote a novel, a supernatural thriller, about a teenage girl who could see ghosts. Her deceased best friend, a ghost named Matthew, haunted an abandoned barn nearby. How I wish my mother could have read it. She enjoyed a good ghost story.

EPILOGUE

"THE FACE OF AN ANGEL" IS HOW SHE DESCRIBED her third-born daughter, Gail, in her memoir. "I was amazed at the beauty of that sweet little child."

She went on to say that they named her Gail Bernice. But Bernice is *my* middle name. *Her* middle name was Marie. Had the chemotherapy drugs muddled my mother's memory? Had time itself? Or was this the same old grief, tears that so long ago had blurred two daughters into one?

When she wrote about the harrowing car accident, the tone and pace of her narrative shifted. Her memory lingered over details and emotions. For several pages, without explanation, she switched the spelling of the other Gail's name to "Gale."

When she described her darkest hour, while baby Gail lay dying in a Montreal hospital, she wrote, "I pleaded with God not to take our child. I was prepared to make a deal with the devil."

And about my birth the following year, she wrote:

"[The doctor] told me he had delivered a goodly number of babies . . . but never had he delivered one where there was not one second of labour and seemingly 'made to order.' Her birth weight was seven pounds, nine ounces. He said it was like a miracle. I replied that it was a miracle and proceeded to tell him of the car accident that took the life of our baby daughter just one year ago. He was deeply moved and said he was privileged to have helped make our prayers become a reality."

Her memoir ended abruptly, right after my birth in the summer of 1956, when she was only twenty-five. Perhaps she felt too ill to continue writing. Or perhaps she had finished telling the story she most needed to tell. The story of her lost child, the one who was waiting for her on the other side.

ACKNOWLEDGMENTS

THANK YOU to my editor at Doubleday Canada, Amy Black, who throughout this too long and sometimes dark process was always a step ahead, encouraging me to go deeper and further when I was convinced, time after time, that I'd already done my best. Thanks to my agent Jackie Kaiser, who has been an invaluable source of practical and wise advice. And sincere gratitude to *The Walrus* and then–senior editor Don Gillmor who, in 2006, encouraged me to submit an essay version of this memoir that had been hiding in my desk drawer for seven years.

I want to thank my sisters and brothers. It can't be easy to sit by while one of seven siblings has the audacity to tell the story of her upbringing, knowing it will profoundly and personally impact them. Each one of you has been kinder than I expected and, I believe, more forgiving. I am deeply grateful.

Finally, thank you with all my heart, Michael and Ben. Ben for long walks and deep conversation, and Michael for his archangel spirit. Living with someone who is tossing about inside a stormy memoir can be a misery, but Michael never complained. Instead he held the boat steady so I could write.